Building an Enduring Peace in Yemen

Lessons from Five Years of RAND Research

DANIEL EGEL, TREVOR JOHNSTON, ASHLEY L. RHOADES, ERIC ROBINSON

RAND

For more information on this publication, visit www.rand.org/t/RRA733-1

Library of Congress Cataloging-in-Publication Data is available for this publication.
ISBN: 978-1-9774-0649-1

Published by the RAND Corporation, Santa Monica, Calif.

Preface

Yemen's civil war, now in its sixth year, has killed more than 250,000 people and created one of the worst humanitarian crises in the world today. From almost the very beginning of the conflict, the international community has tried to broker a peace between the conflict's antagonists. However, these United Nations–led peace talks have struggled to get traction, and, as the conflict has raged on, the antagonists have become increasingly entrenched in their positions.

This report draws on five years of RAND research to describe the challenges facing efforts to achieve an enduring peace in Yemen and to outline how the international community can work constructively to overcome those challenges. This work should be of interest to policymakers in Europe, in the Middle East, in the United States, and at the United Nations who endeavor to establish an enduring peace in Yemen.

The research described in this volume was funded by generous philanthropic contributions to the Center for Middle East Public Policy (CMEPP), part of International Programs at the RAND Corporation. CMEPP brings together analytic excellence and regional expertise from across the RAND Corporation to address the most critical political, social, and economic challenges facing the Middle East today. For more information about CMEPP, visit http://www.rand.org/cmepp.html or contact the center director (contact information is provided on the center's webpage).

This volume draws on a body of previous work for the Office of the Secretary of Defense and the Department of State conducted within the International Security and Defense Policy Center of the RAND National Security Research Division (NSRD). NSRD conducts research and analysis for the Office of the Secretary of Defense, the U.S. Intelligence Community, U.S. State Department, allied foreign governments, and foundations. For more information on the RAND International Security and Defense Policy Center, see www.rand.org/nsrd/isdp or contact the Center director (contact information is provided on the webpage).

Contents

Figures

Summary

The central question motivating this study is deceptively simple: How do you build an enduring peace in Yemen? The short answer: No one knows. Time and again, negotiated cease-fires have proven unsustainable, and once-promising confidence-building measures have failed to change the status quo, let alone achieve an enduring peace.

We draw on five years of RAND Corporation research to provide new insights into this fundamental question. This work includes an expansive data collection effort with four main components, focused on assessing (1) national conflict dynamics, (2) regional influence networks and key actors, (3) local drivers of conflict and sources of resiliency, and (4) international perspectives on what must be done to end the conflict. Our research provides no simple solution to resolve the crisis, but it helps explain the grievances that have gotten us to this point and, more importantly, offers clear recommendations for ending the cycle of violence, failed peace talks, and broken promises.

Yemen's current civil war traces its origins to unresolved historical grievances related to political disenfranchisement and economic marginalization across key communities in Yemen. We trace the decades-long history of these grievances, between south and north, between elites and citizens, and between Yemen's regime and its periphery. These inequalities, more so than other factors, represent the foremost barriers to enduring peace.

The staggering human costs of Yemen's civil war have only exacerbated these inequalities, as is clear from the first component of RAND's data collection effort. Using novel data on national conflict dynamics, we narrate the staggering costs of the conflict in terms of destruction of infrastructure, loss of economic production, and untold costs to human welfare. But this analysis, coupled with other sources of data on the conflict, suggests that certain elites have actually prospered amid the conflict, profiting off the war and the humanitarian aid flowing into Yemen to consolidate their military power and financial strength.

To better understand the incentives of these elites, we draw on an extensive actor-mapping effort across Yemen to diagnose how political influence, economic interests, and military ties have shaped the roles of key actors in the peace process. Although most accounts of the conflict tend to focus on the role of foreign powers, whose complicated interests and support have fueled proxy warfare in Yemen, our research highlights the importance of local elite actors who will be pivotal in future peace negotiations. This research provides a uniquely granular understanding of political dynamics in southern Yemen, where resurgent separatists have threatened the fragile peace process on account of historical grievances. Specifically, our network analysis identifies key actors with constructive roles as mediators, yet still others who will look to spoil any peace agreement.

But our research suggests that enduring peace in Yemen requires much more than peace amongst the country's elites. Rather, peace must be enforced and sustained at the local level for it to become enduring. Drawing on nearly 200 interviews with key military, government, community, and tribal actors across Yemen, we assess that drivers of local conflict in Yemen most often stem from traditional disputes related to Yemen's long history of economic deprivation and limited property rights. Our research suggests that competition for land and other resources is the single most common driver of local conflict. In more-rural areas, such as Shabwa and Hadramawt, these conflicts often stem from tribal clashes over territory with valuable resources. And in more-urban areas, such as Aden and Taiz, local conflicts often stem from neighborhood disputes over contested property lines. However routine these disputes may seem, many are rooted in a long history of insecure and contested property rights in Yemen.

Our research suggests that Yemen's rich tradition of local mediation has flourished during the conflict, often substituting for the state in the midst of civil war and state collapse. Tribal sheiks, community leaders, and other local actors have played an essential role in conflict mediation during the war and will be critical to building and sustaining any eventual peace agreement. Peacebuilding in Yemen is likely to succeed only if it embraces the potential for local mediation to resolve conflicts at the lowest level.

Ultimately, Yemen's most immediate political challenge is clear: Negotiate a settlement and then begin the long, hard process of national reconciliation. We offer a proposal for a phased approach to building enduring peace, drawing on more than 70 interviews with senior U.S. officials, United Nations representatives, Yemeni civil society leaders, academics, and international diplomats from across Europe and the Middle East. An enduring peace requires a coordinated international approach to security and the formation of an international body with the influence, mission, and resources to support what will be a decades-long process of reconciliation, reconstruction, and redevelopment. But for this process to succeed, the international community's contributions must enjoy popular legitimacy within Yemen and be led by an inclusive group of Yemenis capable of speaking constructively on behalf of the country's myriad factions. This body must ultimately provide Yemenis with a clear voice and stake in shaping the future of their country toward a more equitable future if it hopes to achieve an enduring peace.

Acknowledgments

We would like to give our thanks first to the RAND Center for Middle East Public Policy Advisory Board, both for the generous funding that allowed us to complete this analysis and the insightful comments and questions on a preliminary version of our findings. In addition, we offer our appreciation and acknowledgment to the Bureau of Conflict and Stabilization Operations at the U.S. Department of State, which had the initial vision to fund activities in support of a peaceful resolution to the conflict in Yemen and provided funding to RAND's National Security Research Division to collect the myriad data that informed this analysis.

Further, we want to give special thanks to Katie Donahue and Dalia Dassa Kaye for providing advice, guidance, and insight throughout the project. We also wish to thank Ambassador (retired) Gerald M. Feierstein of the Middle East Institute and Linda Robinson of RAND for their insightful reviews of this manuscript, which greatly improved its quality and usefulness for those supporting peacebuilding efforts in Yemen. In addition, Ben Connable provided excellent and constructive feedback on a draft version of this report.

Abbreviations

AQAP	Al-Qaeda in the Arabian Peninsula
STC	Southern Transition Council
UAE	United Arab Emirates
UN	United Nations

1. Introduction

Yemen's civil war has killed more than 250,000 people and created some of the worst famine conditions in the world today. It has become a proxy war between the Iranian-supported Houthis, United Arab Emirates–supported southern separatists, and the Saudi-supported internationally recognized government of Yemen. And despite years of United Nations–brokered negotiations, the antagonists have become increasingly entrenched and their positions seemingly irreconcilable.

The central question motivating this study is deceptively simple: How do you build an enduring peace in Yemen? The short answer: No one knows. Time and again, negotiated cease-fires have proved unsustainable and once-promising confidence-building measures have failed to change the status quo, let alone achieve an enduring peace.

We draw on five years of RAND Corporation research to provide new insights into this fundamental question. This work includes an expansive data collection effort, capturing national conflict dynamics, regional influence networks, local drivers of conflict and sources of resiliency, and international perspectives on what must be done to end the conflict. Our research provides no simple solution to resolve the crisis, but it helps explain the grievances that have gotten us to this point and, more importantly, offers clear recommendations for ending the cycle of violence, failed peace talks, and broken promises.

We begin, in Chapter Two, with a brief history of Yemen, tracing the origins of the conflict. We explain how the civil war is a product of unresolved historical grievances related to the political disenfranchisement and economic marginalization of different communities across Yemen. Then, in Chapter Three, we diagnose the costs of this conflict using RAND's unique data collection effort in Yemen, showing how the costs of conflict have been unevenly borne by some groups and in some parts of the country. In Chapter Four, we use RAND's mapping of key local actors to describe how political influence, economic interests, and military ties have shaped the roles of key actors in the peace process. In Chapter Five, we expand beyond these elites and focus on the underlying drivers of local conflict and the mediation mechanisms used to resolve these conflicts, drawing on 200 interviews with key military, government, community, and tribal actors across Yemen.

Ultimately, we conclude the report in Chapter Six, summarizing the implications of this research for the types of action necessary to build an enduring peace in Yemen. An enduring peace requires a coordinated international approach to security and the formation of an international body with the influence, mission, and resources to support what will be a decades-long process of reconciliation, reconstruction, and redevelopment.

2. Yemen's Civil War: A Tale of Economic and Political Inequality

Yemen's civil war began "officially" in September 2014, when Houthi fighters from northern Yemen seized control of the capital of Sana'a.[1] Within just six months, following a nearly bloodless offensive enabled by support from state and tribal security forces, the Houthis consolidated control over nearly the entire country. With Yemen's government on the verge of defeat, Saudi Arabia entered the war on March 26, 2015. The Saudi-led coalition—deploying air power in support of mercenaries, local militias, and state security forces—has proven unable to roll back the Houthis completely, and ongoing United Nations (UN) efforts to find a peaceful resolution to the conflict have failed.

This chapter explores the origin and trajectory of the civil war, building off of years of RAND research on the conflict. This is a civil war that has its origins in local political and economic grievances, the rise of the Houthis, the violent uprisings of the Arab Spring, and the collapse of the democratic process that emerged from the Arab Spring. And although international actors have played dominant roles in the conflict, local political grievances pushed back, driving the unraveling of the Saudi-led coalition and the failure of the UN-led peace process. The failure of the antagonists to achieve peace has resulted in a Yemeni population that is poorer and with even less opportunity for meaningful political participation. Yet this situation has cemented a new status quo in which some warring elites benefit greatly from simmering violence.

These dual inequalities—political and economic—have shaped the origins and trajectory of Yemen's current civil war. As the war has raged, these inequities have deepened, which we explore in greater detail in the following chapter.

Phase 1: The Prelude to Civil War (1978–2011)

Yemen's ongoing civil war has its roots in a political system that provided neither political nor economic opportunities to its citizens, a set of challenges that date back to at least the 1960s.[2] Such inequities have long been a source of instability in Yemen and played a nearly identical role in Yemen's 1994 civil war. This conflict, which came four years after the unification of what had been the Yemen Arab Republic ("North Yemen") and People's Democratic Republic of

[1] Mohammed Ghobari, "Houthi Rebels Sign Deal with Yemen Parties to Form New Government," Reuters, September 21, 2014.

[2] For a discussion of economic and political inequalities dating back to postcolonial Yemen, see Gerald M. Feierstein, "Yemen: The 60-Year War," in Paul Salem and Ross Harrison, eds., *Escaping the Conflict Trap: Toward Ending Civil Wars in the Middle East*, Washington, D.C.: Middle East Institute, 2019.

Yemen ("South Yemen"), was driven in large part by a perception of "northern aggression" by southerners, including political and economic discrimination.[3]

The current civil war, mirroring the experience of the southerners in the 1990s, has its origins in the political and economic disenfranchisement of citizens in Yemen's northern hinterlands.[4] This disenfranchisement was a key contributor to the rise of the Houthis as a political movement in the 1980s and 1990s,[5] playing an important role in the spread of their physical and later ideological influence throughout northern Yemen during the 2004–2013 time frame (see Figure 2.1). Indeed, despite fighting a series of wars against the central government during the 2004–2010 time frame, the Houthis gradually expanded their ideological influence in areas across Yemen suffering from economic inequity (measured by the poverty rate) and political disenfranchisement (measured by the overall provision of government services).[6]

---

[3] Carlos A. Parodi, Elizabeth Rexford, and Elizabeth Van Wie Davis, "The Silent Demise of Democracy: The Role of the Clinton Administration in the 1994 Yemeni Civil War," *Arab Studies Quarterly*, Vol. 16, No. 4, 1994; Sheila Carapico and Jermera Rone, "Yemen: Human Rights in Yemen During and After the 1994 War," *Human Rights Watch/Middle East*, Vol. 6, No. 1, 1994.

[4] For a discussion of the importance of economic grievances in driving historical conflict in Yemen, see Barbara K. Bodine, "Yemen: Primer and Prescriptions," *PRISM*, Vol. 1, No. 3, 2010.

[5] See Chapter Three in Barak A. Salmoni, Bryce Loidolt, and Madeleine Wells, *Regime and Periphery in Northern Yemen: The Huthi Phenomenon*, Santa Monica, Calif.: RAND Corporation, MG-962-DIA, 2010.

[6] This RAND analysis is based on a statistical analysis of the relationship between the timing of Houthi expansion to a district and a variety of socioeconomic characteristics, including poverty, access to services (measured by school enrollment), percentage of the population that is Shia, tribal composition, and population size. Timing of Houthi expansion is based on a systematic review of Yemeni newspaper reporting (in Arabic) that mentions Houthi physical or ideological influence (see the note to Figure 2.1).

Figure 2.1. Houthi Geographic Expansion

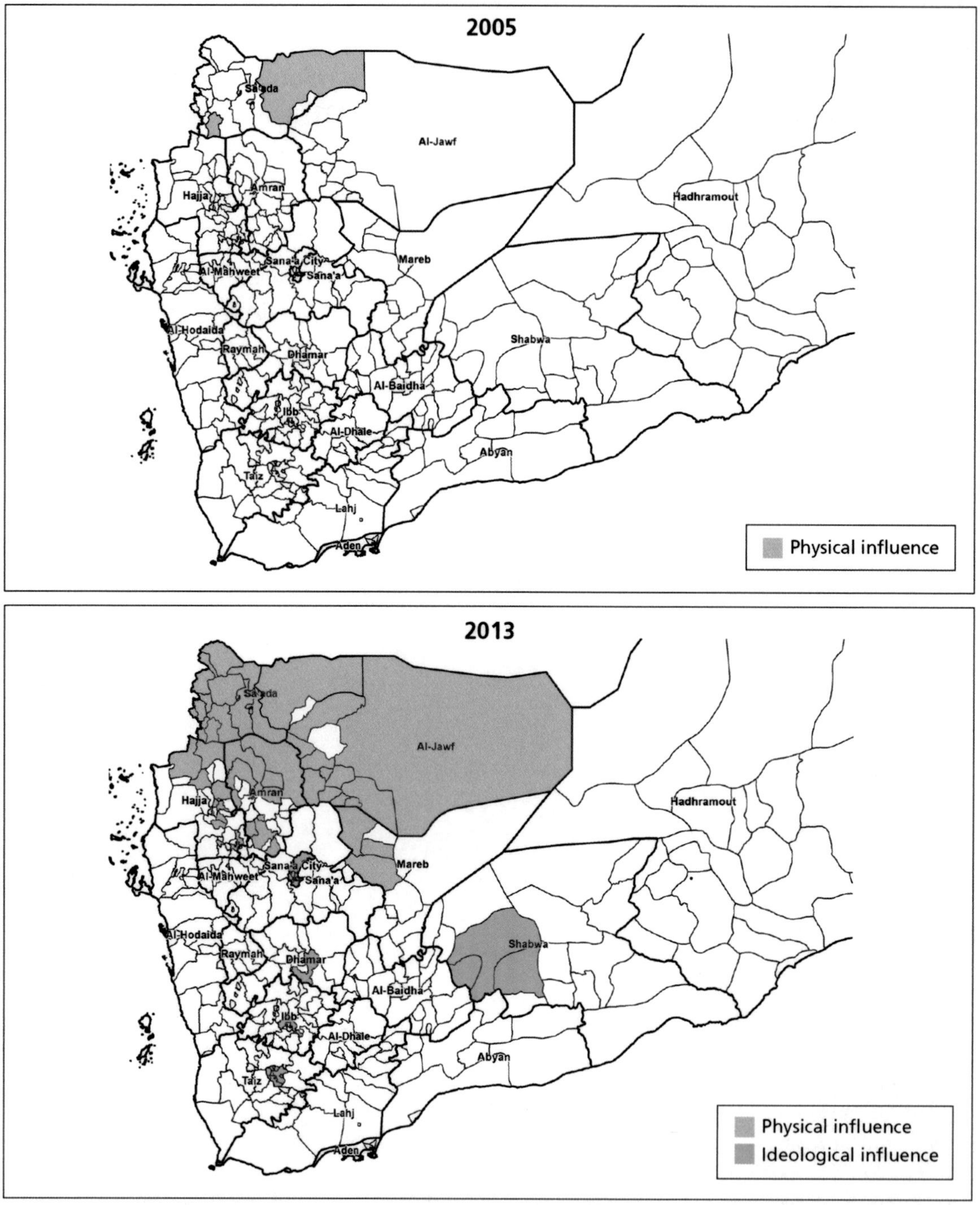

NOTES: To create this figure, we conducted a systematic review of online Yemeni sources (in Arabic) from 2004 to 2013. Houthis are assessed to have physical influence in a district if newspapers discuss violence, roadblocks, indoctrination, or parallel governance associated with the Houthis in a specific district. A district is assessed to have Houthi ideological influence if non-Houthi groups in a district use Houthi rhetoric or engage on pro-Houthi protests or rallies.

Economic and political frustrations set the stage for what would become nationwide popular uprisings in early 2011, in the wake of the collapse of first the Tunisian and then the Egyptian government during the Arab Spring. On the eve of this crisis, the inability of the government to provide either economic opportunities or meaningful political participation had led to a situation in which the "unity and viability of the Yemeni state itself" was under threat.[7] In fact, even before the Arab Spring, in 2009, a combination of high unemployment, dwindling oil revenues, and blossoming frustration with endemic political corruption had driven calls for a national dialogue for political reform.[8] In January 2011, youth and civil society actors poured into the streets of major cities across the country, demanding change in the dysfunctional government and its inability to provide economic opportunities.[9]

Phase 2: A Failed Democratic Process (2011–2014)

In November 2011, following ten months of protests in which youth and civil society were soon joined by "key political parties, power brokers, and tribal actors,"[10] Yemen began a historic democratic process. In an agreement brokered by the Gulf Cooperation Council, Yemen's president of 33 years, Ali Abdullah Saleh, resigned, and the political parties agreed to a two-year period of political transition. A key part of this agreement was the National Dialogue Conference, a ten-month process that began in March 2013, that was intended to result in a new functional, representative, and inclusive government.

But as the National Dialogue Conference drew to a close in January 2014, it became clear that Yemen's democratic experiment was foundering. This process, despite its initial promise, had failed in several major ways. First, the transitional government, led by President Abdrabbuh Mansur Hadi, had done little to address the economic conditions that had inspired nationwide protests three years earlier.[11] Second, the process had failed to address the political grievances of southern Yemenis, who had long been discriminated against and marginalized.[12] Likewise, the process failed to account for similar grievances driving growth in the popular appeal of the Houthi movement among northern Yemenis, including Sunnis.[13]

Critically, this failure was not because the National Dialogue Conference failed to identify these issues but rather because there was not sufficient political will among the parties to drive

---

[7] April Longley Alley, "Tracking the 'Arab Spring': Yemen Changes Everything . . . and Nothing," *Journal of Democracy*, Vol. 24, No. 4, October 2013.

[8] April Longley Allen, "Yemen's Multiple Crises," *Journal of Democracy*, Vol. 21, No. 4, October 2010.

[9] Erica Gaston, *Process Lessons Learned in Yemen's National Dialogue*, Washington, D.C.: United States Institute of Peace, February 2014, p. 2.

[10] Gaston, 2014, p. 2.

[11] E.g., Maged al-Madhaji, *How Yemen's Post-2011 Transitional Phase Ended in War*, Sana'a, Yemen: Sana'a Center for Strategic Studies, May 19, 2016.

[12] E.g., Charles Schmitz, *Yemen's National Dialogue*, Washington, D.C.: Middle East Institute, February 2014.

[13] We thank Ambassador (retired) Gerald M. Feierstein for this helpful observation, highlighting that such grievances were not unique to Yemen's southern governorates.

needed reform. Despite the inclusive nature of the National Dialogue Conference, members of Yemen's political elite played a central role in steering the outcome of this process.[14] However, if they had not, international experience suggests that they might have simply ignored or undermined the outputs of the process.[15] Either way, this outcome was a stark reminder that Yemen's political elite, now including actors from what was once considered Yemen's "periphery,"[16] had captured and capitalized on the early zeal of Yemen's Arab Spring protests. Future efforts for political reform in Yemen must take these challenges into account in designing an inclusive transition process compatible with existing power structures.

Phase 3: Civil War and Political Infighting (2014–Present)

The failures of this political process laid the foundation for the ensuing civil war. The return of protesters to the streets set the stage for the Houthi capture of the capital of Sana'a in September 2014. The transitional government collapsed four months later, when President Hadi fled Sana'a to the southern port city of Aden, and Houthi forces began to march south toward Aden in February 2015.[17] Aided and abetted by tribal and state security forces loyal to former President Saleh, the Houthi's erstwhile adversary, the Houthis rapidly seized control of Taiz (Yemen's third-largest city), Aden's civilian airport, and even a joint U.S.-Yemeni counterterrorism facility along the way.[18] By late March of 2015, the Houthis and their allied forces had encircled Aden and stood poised to consolidate their control over the entire country.[19]

With Aden on the verge of capture and Saudi Arabia fearful that the Houthis would consolidate control over all of Yemen, a Saudi-led coalition began military operations against the Houthis on March 25, 2015.[20] In the early days of the intervention, the coalition relied heavily on airpower to degrade Houthi military capabilities, helping slow their advance in the south. Over time, however, as the Houthi positions became entrenched across key strategic locations and the major battle lines between the two sides of the conflict became largely fixed, ground forces became increasingly important to the war effort.

---

[14] Thania Paffenholz and Nick Ross, "Inclusive Political Settlements: New Insights from Yemen's National Dialogue," *PRISM*, Vol. 6, No. 1, March 2016.

[15] Thania Paffenholz and Nick Ross, "Inclusive Peace Processes—an Introduction," presented at *Development Dialogue 2015*, Hubli, India, February 6–8, 2015.

[16] Schmitz, 2014.

[17] BBC, "President Hadi Leaves Yemen as Saudi-Led Raids Continue," March 27, 2015.

[18] Michael Knights and Alex Almeida, "The Saudi-UAE War Effort in Yemen (Part 1): Operation Golden Arrow in Aden," Washington Institute, August 10, 2015.

[19] Sami Aboudi, "Allies of Yemen Houthis Seize Aden Airport, Close In on President," Reuters, March 25, 2015.

[20] Mark Mazzetti and David D. Kirkpatrick, "Saudi Arabia Leads Air Assault in Yemen," *New York Times*, March 25, 2015.

Political infighting among the civil war's antagonists was quick to emerge. For the Houthis, the most dramatic internal rivalry developed with loyalists to former President Saleh. For nearly a decade, the Houthis waged an insurgency against the Saleh regime, which had long repressed the Zaidi community in the north. But in an extraordinary about-face, former President Saleh joined forces with the Houthis in July 2016 in an ill-fated attempt to reassert his power. This expedient alliance underlined the shrewd political calculus that had defined the former president's rule.[21] However, fissures soon began to emerge between Saleh loyalists and Houthi fighters, driving an already fragile alliance toward failure.[22] Ultimately, Saleh loyalists' struggle for political control culminated in the assassination of the former president by the Houthis in December 2017.

Ultimately, political infighting within the Houthi movement would become a persistent phenomenon of the crisis, as the group "reconfigured the local political environment[,] . . . stirring opposition from increasingly marginalized elites and allies."[23] By 2019, internal factions within the Houthi leadership had become increasingly apparent, as had their limited ability to control rank-and-file Houthi fighters operating throughout the country.[24]

The divisions were even more pronounced among the Saudi-led coalition. During the early years of the conflict, the Houthi threat united an unusual coalition that combined Emirati-backed southern separatists and the remnants of Yemen's internationally recognized government under Hadi. Major fissures in this coalition began to emerge almost as soon as the foreign intervention began in 2015. By early 2017, escalating tensions even led Hadi to accuse the United Arab Emirates (UAE)—a key supporter of the coalition's efforts across the south—of "behaving like an occupier of Yemen rather than its liberator."[25] In the months and years that followed, long-standing regional, political, and personal grievances led to violent clashes between the Saudi- and the Emirati-backed factions.[26]

This infighting came to a head in 2018, when the southern separatists, under the unified banner of the recently established Southern Transition Council (STC), seized control of the

---

[21] Saleh's regime marginalized large swathes of the population while cultivating relationships with powerful local actors, such as the prominent tribes near Sana'a, who could advance the president's interests.

[22] For a discussion of the fragility of the Houthi-Saleh alliance at the time, see Gerald M. Feierstein, "Resolving the Conflict in Yemen: U.S. Interests, Risks, and Policy," testimony before the U.S. Senate Foreign Relations Committee on March 9, 2017, Washington, D.C.: Middle East Institute, 2017.

[23] Andrea Carboni and Luca Nevola, "Inside Ibb: A Hotbed of Infighting in Houthi-Controlled Yemen," Armed Conflict Location and Event Data Project, October 3, 2019.

[24] As an example, in late 2019, when one of the Houthis' military arms in Sana'a detained and then tortured a UN employee, it took multiple days before senior Houthi leadership was able to identify even who had detained the individual.

[25] David Hearst, "Yemen President Says UAE Acting Like Occupiers," *Middle East Eye*, May 12, 2017.

[26] Middle East Policy Council, "Yemen's Anti-Houthi Alliance Cracking from Within," August 20, 2019; Sudarsan Raghavan, "In Ancient Yemeni City, Violence Turns Inward," *Washington Post*, December 6, 2018; *Gulf News*, "Unity in Defeating Al Houthi Scourge," August 11, 2019.

internationally recognized government's headquarters in Yemen. The STC ejected the Hadi government completely from its capital in exile, Aden, in August 2019 and was implicated in a number of attacks against Yemeni security forces.[27]

Phase 4: A Struggling Peace Process (2015–Present)

Even as fighting has raged on, the international community and influential local figures have been engaged in an ongoing effort to bring peace to Yemen through UN-led peace talks. But these talks have struggled to get traction. The first round of negotiations in Geneva in 2015 proved inconclusive, with the two parties refusing to even sit together.[28]

And none of the cease-fires brokered by the UN would prove enduring. The first such cease-fire, in December 2015, was almost immediately violated by both parties to the conflict.[29] They were similarly involved in "serious violations" of the next cease-fire, which collapsed in August 2016 after a tenuous four months of peace talks in Kuwait.[30] Subsequent cease-fires would often collapse within 48–72 hours of their initiation.

By 2018, UN efforts had devolved toward crisis management, rather than producing real progress toward peace.[31] The Stockholm Agreement signed in December 2018, though celebrated by some as a restart to negotiations, was largely a stopgap measure to stem Yemen's deepening humanitarian crisis.[32] In late 2019, in a Saudi-led effort that culminated in the Riyadh Agreement, the international community pivoted to the task of brokering reconciliation between coalition allies. This effort faltered and ultimately failed as well.[33]

---

[27] Reuters, "Yemeni Separatists Arrest Dozens of Government Loyalists in Aden," August 31, 2019.

[28] BBC, "Yemen Crisis: Geneva Talks Fail to Produce Ceasefire," June 19, 2015.

[29] Nick Cumming-Bruce, "Yemen Agrees to Cease-Fire with Rebels as Peace Talks Begin," *New York Times*, December 15, 2015; Kareem Fahim and Saeed Al-Batati, "Yemen Peace Talks End with No End to Conflict," *New York Times*, December 20, 2015; Stephen W. Day, "Why Yemen's Peace Talks Failed," *Washington Post*, July 7, 2015. The most promising effort, a UN-brokered cessation of hostilities that lasted from April to August 2016, was marred by violations and collapsed following a coalition strike against a health facility (United Nations, "UN Officials Welcome Cessation of Hostilities," *UN News*, April 11, 2016a; United Nations, "Ban Condemns Reported Coalition Airstrike on Rural Hospital That Leaves 11 Dead," *UN News*, August 16, 2016b).

[30] United Nations, "Yemen: UN Envoy Urges 72-Hour Extension of Ceasefire," *UN News*, October 22, 2016c; Reuters, "U.N.-Sponsored Peace Talks for Yemen," June 7, 2018.

[31] Ibrahim Jalal, "From Stockholm to Riyadh: Breaking the Yemen Peace Process Deadlock," Middle East Institute, February 13, 2020b.

[32] Peter Salisbury, "What Does the Stockholm Agreement Mean for Yemen?" *Washington Post*, December 21, 2018b.

[33] The Riyadh Agreement, signed on November 5, 2019, was designed to reunite the internationally recognized Yemen government and southern separatists. As part of the agreement, Emirati forces pulled out of Aden and southern Yemen and ceded control to the Saudis. Fighting in the south temporarily abated but soon flared again as the deal failed to reconcile the conflicting visions of the Emirati-backed southern separatists (who remained intent on secession) and the Saudi-backed government of Yemen (which sought to remain in power and keep the north and south unified). See Helen Lackner, "Yemen: Why the Riyadh Agreement Is Collapsing," European Council on

The intransigence of the parties to this conflict, and their inability to make the sacrifices needed to achieve peace, has resulted in a Yemeni population that is poorer and with even less opportunity for meaningful political participation. Even as the conflict has created an unprecedented humanitarian crisis, highlighted in stark relief by the inability of the UN to broker safe passage for humanitarian assistance into the critical port in Hodeidah,[34] there are many who benefit from Yemen's new status quo. These uneven costs of the conflict are the focus of the next chapter.

Foreign Relations, February 3, 2020; Helen Lackner and Raiman Al-Hamdani, "War and Pieces: Political Divides in Southern Yemen," European Council on Foreign Relations, January 22, 2020.

[34] Ibrahim Jalal, "Yemen's Stockholm Agreement One Year On: Imaginary Progress?" Middle East Institute, January 22, 2020a.

3. The Uneven Costs of the Conflict

The human costs of Yemen's civil war have been staggering, with more than 250,000 killed by the violence or the disease and famine resulting from that violence. Yet a small but influential group of Yemenis has benefited from this simmering conflict. These war "beneficiaries," a blend of Yemen's traditional elite and many newcomers to Yemen's national stage, have exploited the instability and foreign assistance of all types for economic and political gain.

Understanding the winners and losers in the ongoing civil war is critical in designing effective and durable solutions to the current conflict. This chapter provides a national-level perspective on these winners and losers, by combining insights from interviews with local Yemeni actors and a nationwide data collection effort (designed and led by RAND) that provided real-time insights into nearly 13,000 separate incidents of fighting, mobilization of forces, civil unrest, peaceful protests, and local mediation efforts (see Figure 3.1).

Figure 3.1. Violent Events and Local Mediations in RAND's Conflict Incident Data

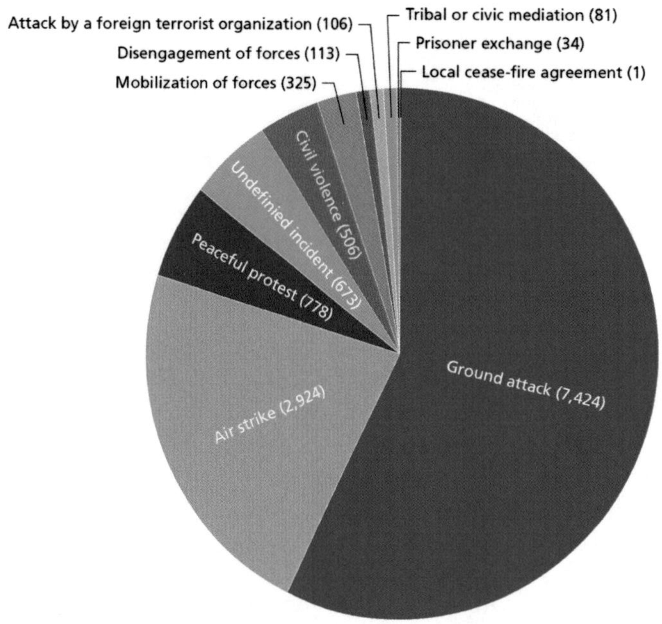

NOTES: N = 12,965. All data were collected by RAND partners in Yemen between July 2017 and May 2018, using local media reporting. No data were collected in Al-Mahrah governorate.

This chapter focuses first on the direct implications of the fighting and then examines the conflict from the perspective of food access and health, the two sectors that have been the focus of international humanitarian assistance.

Elites Have Prospered Amid the Fighting

More than 110,000 Yemenis have been killed as a direct result of fighting during the civil war, including at least 12,000 civilians.[35] The violence has been concentrated in the governorates along the front lines of the conflict (shown in Figure 3.2), where total fatalities from violence have often exceeded 4 percent of the adult male population.

These staggeringly high death tolls in some parts of Yemen have often devastated entire communities. In Al-Jawf (6.5 percent) and Marib (8.4 percent), military offensives by both the Houthis and the Saudi-led coalition are both to blame for the extremely high fatality rates. In northernmost Saada (4.5 percent), the bulk of lives lost to the conflict so far have been the result of coalition operations and air strikes against the Houthi movement's historical homeland.[36]

Figure 3.2. The Human Cost of Yemen's Civil War

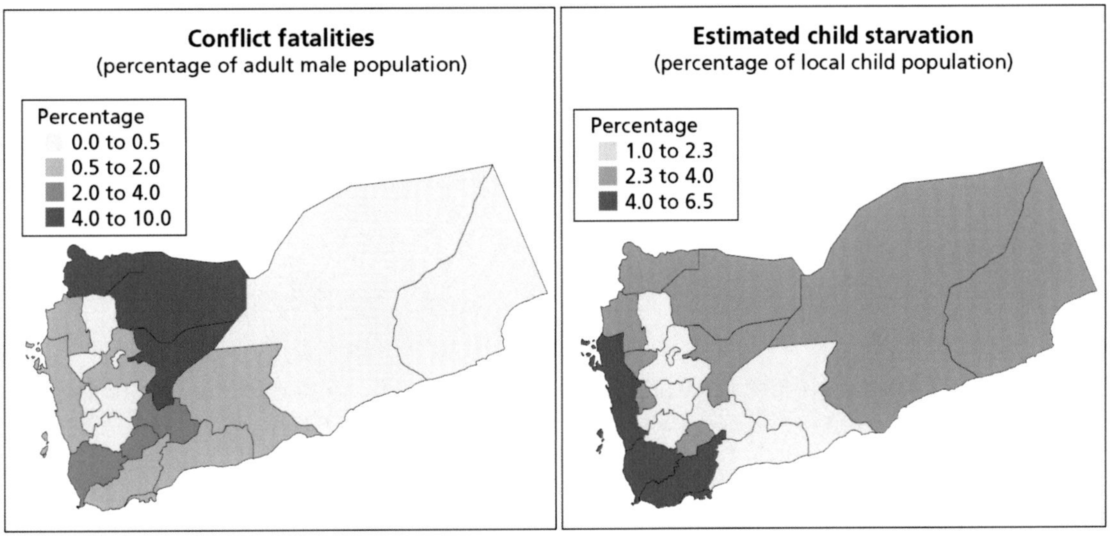

SOURCES: The figure in the left panel is based on estimates of the total conflict fatalities from Armed Conflict Location and Event Data Project (ACLED) (current as of March 7, 2010; see Clionadh Raleigh, Andrew Linke, Håvard Hegre, and Joakim Karlsen, "Introducing ACLED-Armed Conflict Location and Event Data," *Journal of Peace Research*, Vol. 47, No. 5, 2010), and estimates of the adult male population are from the Yemen Central Statistical Organization (current as of 2017; see Yemen Central Statistical Organization, "Yemen—CSO 2017 Population Projections by Governorate & District, Sex & Age Disaggregated," data set, Data.world, last updated 2019). In the right panel, estimates of the total child starvation are based on the approach used by Save the Children (Save the Children, "Yemen: Hunger and Disease Could Kill at Least 50,000 Children This Year, More If Aid Blockade Continues," press release, November 15, 2017; Save the Children, "Yemen: 85,000 Children May Have Died from Starvation Since Start of War," November 20, 2018). The geographic distribution is determined according to food insecurity data from the UN Office for the Coordination of Humanitarian Affairs nutrition smart survey, and child population estimates are from the same source (United Nations Office for the Coordination of Humanitarian Affairs, "Yemen—Nutrition Smart Survey," data set, 2019).

---

[35] Sam Jones and Matthias Sulz, "Press Release: Over 100,000 Reported Killed in Yemen War," Armed Conflict Location and Event Data Project, October 31, 2019.

[36] Overall governorate-specific fatality rates are based on data from ACLED that spans 2015–present, while the propensity of different aggressors is from RAND's conflict incident data spanning 2017–2018.

Although the average Yemenis along the front lines of these conflicts have suffered, ongoing violence has actually benefited a small group of individuals among the leadership on both sides of the conflict. Foremost among these beneficiaries is a small group of political elites among the Houthis who have gradually consolidated their political control of Yemen's northern governorates.[37] Houthi military commanders have profited significantly from the conflict as well, leveraging their physical control over key economic resources in the north for personal financial gain, including customs facilities and fuel import infrastructure.[38] Such economic profiteering by military commanders has often disrupted traditional power structures within Yemen's warring parties, particularly so within the Houthi movement.[39]

Fatalities have been comparably lower in Yemen's southern governorates, where fighting has been more episodic, but this has not prevented key elites from taking advantage of the conflict to further their political and economic control. The growing influence of the Emirati-backed STC is perhaps the most notable, as it has transformed a group of formerly marginalized southern separatists into one of the most powerful political forces in the south. However, many of the key political and security actors in southern Yemen now benefit personally from the status quo, as a result of direct financial support from Saudi Arabia or the UAE and the ensuing political influence associated with such support.[40]

Humanitarian Impacts

Beyond the direct consequences of the violence, at least 150,000 children age five and under have died from starvation as a consequence of the conflict.[41] This is equivalent to 3 percent of the total number of young children nationwide. Moreover, as illustrated in Figure 3.2, an

---

[37] We determined this using conversations with in-country contacts, although Peter Salisbury comes to a similar conclusion (Peter Salisbury, *Yemen: National Chaos, Local Order*, London: Chatham House, December 2017, p. 28).

[38] Salisbury, 2017, p. 28; Sana'a Center for Strategic Studies, "Yemen's War Profiteers Are Potential Spoilers of the Peace Process," December 11, 2018.

[39] For a deeper discussion on the Houthi movement, its structure, and divisions within the organization, see Trevor Johnston, Matthew Lane, Abigail Casey, Heather J. Williams, Ashley L. Rhoades, James Sladden, Nathan Vest, Jordan R. Reimer, and Ryan Haberman, *Could the Houthis Be the Next Hizballah? Iranian Proxy Development in Yemen and the Future of the Houthi Movement*, Santa Monica, Calif.: RAND Corporation, RR-2551-OSD, 2020.

[40] In Chapter Four, we return to this topic in greater depth, discussing a series of southern secessionists and militants whose prominence, influence, and wealth have increased significantly over the course of the conflict. For several of these actors, this growth has depended on the support foreign patrons, most notably Saudi Arabia and the UAE. Other actors, however, have reportedly drawn support from Oman and Qatar as well.

[41] This estimate is based on two analyses by Save the Children, with the 2018 release ("85,000 Children May Have Died from Starvation Since Start of War") providing an estimate for the first 43 months of the conflict and the 2017 release ("Yemen: Hunger and Disease Could Kill at Least 50,000 Children This Year, More If Aid Blockade Continues") giving us a rate that we used to extrapolate the remaining 17 months. The geographic distribution of the total number of estimated deaths is based on the severe acute malnutrition prevalence in the most recent SMART Survey (United Nations Office for the Coordination of Humanitarian Affairs, 2019; see Figure 3).

estimated 4 percent or more of children in each of Yemen's highly populous coastal lowland governorates—notionally under the protection of the Saudi-led coalition—have died from starvation. And many more children suffer from stunting and wasting caused by the severe food insecurity now affecting more than one-third of the population.[42] These children, and their communities, will live with the consequences of today's crisis for years to come.

This humanitarian crisis is largely not the result of insufficient quantities of food;[43] rather, it is a consequence of key actions made by the conflict's antagonists. The dramatic food insecurity in the coastal areas has been attributed largely to coalition air strikes,[44] which reportedly deliberately targeted critical transportation infrastructure and food production, storage, and distribution capabilities.[45] RAND's conflict-mapping efforts demonstrate the intensity of the coalition air campaign in Figure 3.3, particularly along Yemen's western coast. This includes more than 460 airstrikes conducted in ten months alone between late 2017 and mid-2018 in Hodeidah, home of the primary port through which humanitarian goods arrive in Yemen.

Like the violence itself, the worsening food crisis has had clear beneficiaries. The clearest beneficiary is again the Houthis, who have seized as much as $350 million in food aid per year provided by the international community to address local famines.[46] RAND's conflict incident data provide clear evidence that the Houthis diverted food shipments from humanitarian organizations for Houthis' own use hundreds of times.

The fighting has also devastated Yemen's health infrastructure. In addition to ongoing shortages of medicines, equipment, and staff resulting from the civil war, the coalition and Houthis have collectively been involved in more than 150 attacks against health facilities.[47] Yemen's weakened health care system, which has been operating at an estimated 50 percent capacity for years,[48] has dramatically affected marginalized Yemenis. A cholera epidemic, the

---

[42] United Nations, "10 Million Yemenis 'One Step Away from Famine,' UN Food Relief Agency Calls for 'Unhindered Access' to Frontline Regions," *UN News*, March 26, 2019.

[43] V TLR, "Yemen: Questions About an Aid System," Fondation Médecins Sans Frontières, Centre de Réflexion sur l'Action et les Savoirs Humanitaires, June 20, 2019.

[44] Global Rights Compliance and World Peace Foundation, *Accountability for Mass Starvation: Starvation in Yemen*, Den Haag, Netherlands; Somerville, Mass., September 3, 2019.

[45] Iona Craig, "Bombed into Famine: How Saudi Air Campaign Targets Yemen's Food Supplies," *The Guardian*, December 12, 2017.

[46] David Beasley from the World Food Programme is quoted as saying that "at least 10 percent of the $175 million of food aid per month they provided was being diverted in Houthi areas to help fund the conflict" (Michael Holden, "WFP Hopeful Yemen's 'Good' Houthis Will Prevail to Allow Food Aid Suspension to End," Reuters, June 21, 2019).

[47] United Nations Department of Global Communications, "Regular Press Briefing by the Information Service: Syria, Yemen, World Migration Trends," November 15, 2019.

[48] International Rescue Committee, *They Die of Bombs, We Die of Need: Impact of Collapsing Public Health Systems in Yemen*, New York, March 26, 2018.

world's largest in recorded history,[49] is one of the many consequences, having resulted in more than 2.3 million cases and nearly 4,000 dead.[50]

Figure 3.3. Air Strikes Reported in RAND's Conflict Incident Data, 2017–2018

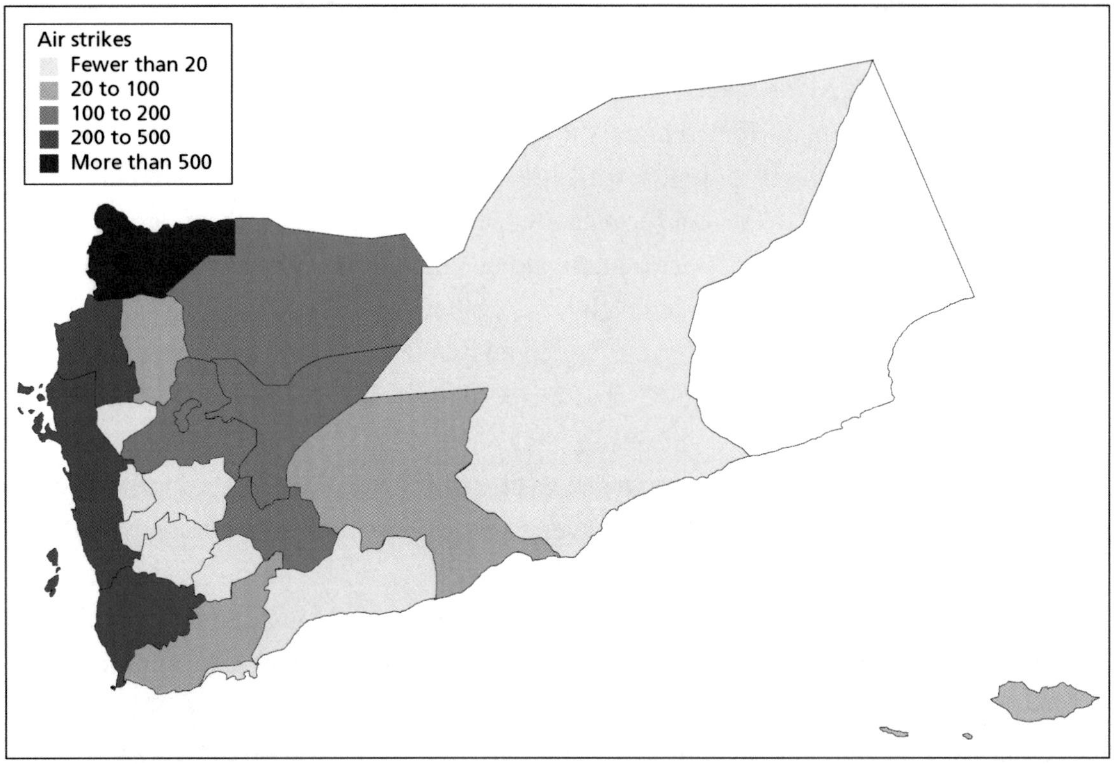

NOTES: *N* = 2,924. All data were collected by RAND partners in Yemen between July 2017 and May 2018, using local media reporting. No data were collected in Al-Mahrah governorate.

Tremendous support from the international community to address this health crisis, at nearly $750 million for 2019 only, has also created opportunities for manipulation.[51] Both the Houthis and Yemeni government security forces have been implicated in stealing humanitarian medical supplies for their own use.[52] And both sides are increasingly placing restrictions on the activities

---

[49] Christina Potter, "Largest Cholera Outbreak on Record Continues," Outbreak Observatory, January 16, 2020.

[50] World Health Organization, "Cholera Situation in Yemen, December 2019," December 31, 2019.

[51] This figure includes total funding for the health, nutrition, and WASH (water, sanitation, and hygiene) clusters for 2019; see United Nations Financial Tracking Service, "Yemen 2019," webpage, undated.

[52] For a Houthi-specific discussion, see Maggie Michael, "UN Probes Corruption in Its Own Agencies in Yemen Aid Effort," Associated Press, August 5, 2019. For a Yemeni government–specific discussion, see Mark Lowcock, "Briefing to the Security Council on the Humanitarian Situation in Yemen," United Nations Office for the Coordination of Humanitarian Affairs, February 18, 2020.

of humanitarian aid agencies, raising significant concerns that these groups are using this assistance to advance their own political objectives.[53]

In addition, both the Houthis and the Saudi-backed Yemeni government have been implicated in weaponizing the financial system to their own political advantage, which is increasingly impoverishing Yemenis and exacerbating the humanitarian crisis.[54] The Yemeni rial has lost more than one-half its value since the beginning of the conflict, dramatically reducing the wealth and buying power of regular Yemenis. But the erosion of the rial's value has enriched political elites and financiers on both sides of the conflict through currency arbitrage.[55]

The benefit accruing to a small number of influential elites on both sides of the conflict stands in stark relief to the vast humanitarian impacts of this crisis. It is also a reason why the various factions have proved willing to prolong the conflict, and negotiate in bad faith, for so long.[56] The complex network of political and security actors in Yemen's southern governorates and the implications of their financial and personal allegiances to foreign powers and each other are the focus of the analysis in the subsequent chapter.

---

[53] Lowcock, 2020.

[54] This impoverishing effect has been seen most dramatically in food security, as loss of buying power is one of the primary contributors to food insecurity (Global Rights Compliance and World Peace Foundation, 2019, p. 5).

[55] Sana'a Center for Strategic Studies, "Yemen Economic Bulletin: How Currency Arbitrage Has Reduced the Funds Available to Address the Humanitarian Crisis," September 6, 2017; *Middle East Eye*, "Yemen's Rial Plummets as Government and Houthis Battle over Banknotes," January 9, 2020.

[56] The inference in the sentence is our own, although Salisbury (2017, pp. 48–49) comes to a similar conclusion in a detailed analysis of the incentives of different actors to participate in the peace process. He concludes that there is a strong incentive for the Houthis, STC, and others to "spoil" negotiations and maintain the status quo.

4. The Unresolved Southern Question: Political and Economic Challenges to Peacebuilding

Peacebuilding in Yemen depends on winning over an ever-changing mix of actors with complicated political histories and competing economic interests. Over the past five years, the international community, led by the Office of the Special Envoy of the Secretary-General for Yemen, has mediated tough negotiations between Houthi and Hadi-aligned representatives in hopes of building a sustainable cease-fire. Through these negotiations, UN mediators have created a venue for the warring sides to exchange their political, economic, and security demands, helping clarify some of these interests and representing an important step toward peace. Although these initiatives have occasionally enjoyed mild success, peace remains elusive.

In this chapter, we discuss several of the major challenges to peacebuilding in Yemen, focusing on the underlying and unresolved political and economic grievances in southern Yemen. Drawing on RAND's actor-mapping research conducted across Yemen,[57] we explore these challenges and highlight key actors whose personal rivalries, political ties, and economic interests illustrate the difficulties of negotiating an enduring peace agreement. Although some of these actors have the potential to help reconcile Yemen's divisions, many are just as likely to play the role of spoiler, threatening the peace process.

This chapter suggests that, although southerners may have a shared cause, they lack a common vision for their future. Winning over these restive areas is critical to achieving an enduring peace for Yemen, which will depend on the support of local actors who enjoy wide respect and influence. If the peace process is to succeed, it must be more inclusive and address the long-standing political and economic grievances that shape the power of these elites across Yemen's southern governorates.

The Rise of the South and the Collapse of the Coalition

Since the civil war began, the conflict has largely been framed as one fought between the Houthis, who control most of the areas historically composing North Yemen, and the Saudi-led coalition forces, who control most of southern Yemen and claim Aden as their capital. Despite this framing, the coalition has long been riven by entrenched divisions that go back decades and

[57] In 2017, RAND began a collaboration with research partners on the ground in Yemen with experience analyzing political, economic, tribal, and community dynamics throughout the country, across the political spectrum. These partners leveraged local relationships to engage with key stakeholders across ten governorates in Yemen to produce a highly granular mapping of regional powerbrokers and influencers. This research focused on identifying influential local actors who could play important roles, both positive and negative, in the peace process. After identifying these actors, we developed a series of network models that mapped their cross-cutting relationships, helping unpack local political dynamics and better informing efforts to build broad coalitions in support of the peace process.

are rooted in historical grievances around southern political disenfranchisement and economic marginalization.

Perhaps no individual better illustrates these deep-rooted grievances and their effects on the peace process than Aidarous Al-Zubaidi, the current president of the STC (see Figure 4.1). Al-Zubaidi only recently entered the national political stage, having previously led armed separatist groups in Ad-Dhale'a. Despite its small population size, the governorate's central location, historical importance in southern politics,[58] and relatively large number of fighters makes Ad-Dhale'a integral to the peace process. Al-Zubaidi and others from Ad-Dhale'a have long criticized the central government for marginalizing southern Yemen. Many of these historical grievances, which revolved around political disenfranchisement and the "distribution of oil wealth and land,"[59] persist to this day and continue to breed distrust and enmity within the Saudi-led coalition.

Figure 4.1. Profile of Aidarous Al-Zubaidi

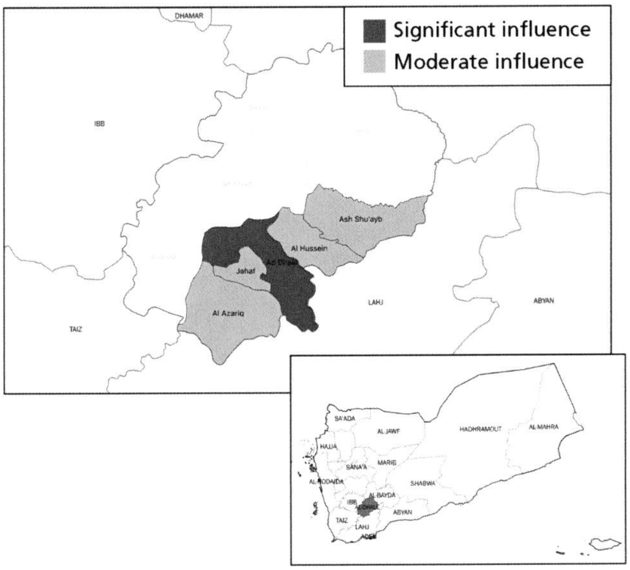

Name: Aidarous Al-Zubaidi
(Arabic: عيدروس الزبيدي)

Current and past positions: President of the STC (May 2017–present), governor of Aden (December 2015–April 2017)

Major areas of influence: Ad-Dhale'a, Aden

Personal history, political allies, and interests: Al-Zubaidi is a long-time militant secessionist who entered national politics only recently, having spent nearly a decade leading armed separatist activities in Ad-Dhale'a against successive Sana'a-based governments. Since 2015, his influence has grown dramatically with the formation of the STC. Drawing on support from the UAE and local actors, Al-Zubaidi has become the most influential leader in the south.

Given this history, Al-Zubaidi's place in the coalition has created tension since the beginning, but his forces were essential early on in resisting the Houthi advance. At the beginning of the war, Al-Zubaidi and other southern leaders initially avoided joining the conflict.

---

[58] More than a decade before the formation of the STC, a broader umbrella secessionist movement, Hirak, was founded in Ad-Dhale'a (Lackner and al-Hamdani, 2020).

[59] James Reinl, "Yemen Won't See Peace Without Addressing Southern Demands: Separatist Leader," *Middle East Eye*, December 15, 2018.

However, he soon saw the civil war as an opportunity to help achieve an independent south Yemen. As the Houthis began their advance across southern governorates, resistance groups from Ad-Dhale'a joined the conflict and were able to retake the governorate relatively quickly, earning Al-Zubaidi wider respect and prestige. This victory was all the more impressive because fighters from Ad-Dhale'a did not depend on UAE assistance and were widely seen as "among the best-organized and effective fighters in the south."[60] Hadi rewarded Al-Zubaidi by appointing him governor of Aden in December 2015. Al-Zubaidi quickly became one of the most powerful figures in Aden, and he has since expanded his influence throughout southern Yemen.

But Al-Zubaidi was hardly the only southern leader whose fortunes rose with his success fighting the Houthis. Hani Bin Buraik, a prominent Salafi sheikh, also grew his influence during these early months of the war and translated that influence into an official position within the Hadi government, becoming a state minister in January 2016 (see Figure 4.2). When the Saudi-led coalition intervened in March 2015, Bin Buraik became the UAE's first point of contact on the ground, managing relationships with resistance fighters and other militia groups in Aden.[61] Bin Buraik has been described as a "staunch UAE ally,"[62] whose prominence is closely tied to his informal leadership over the Security Belt Forces, a paramilitary group that comprises a mix of Salafi and southern resistance fighters trained and equipped by the UAE.[63]

Figure 4.2. Profile of Hani Bin Buraik

Name: Hani Bin Buraik (Arabic: هاني بن بريك)

Current and past positions: Vice president of the STC (May 2017–present), state minister (January 2016–April 2017)

Major areas of influence: Aden

Personal history, political allies, and interests: Bin Buraik has direct influence over the Security Belt Forces, making him one of the most important security actors in much of the south. Born and raised in Aden, Bin Buraik later took part in the fighting against the Houthis between 2011 and 2013. During this time, Bin Buraik widened his network and opened a direct line of communication with Saudi intelligence. Saudi Arabia stopped dealing with Bin Buraik as the divide grew between Saudi Arabia and the UAE over their competing visions for Yemen and, in particular, the south.

---

[60] Peter Salisbury, *Yemen's Southern Powder Keg*, London: Chatham House, March 2018a, p. 16.

[61] On its first visit to Aden during the war, the UAE, which oversaw the battle to retake Aden, sent 16 Emirati officers to meet Bin Buraik at his own house (according to RAND actor-mapping data from 2017).

[62] Salisbury, 2018a, p. 21.

[63] Although estimates vary widely, the Security Belt Forces likely number around 15,000, but some sources report up to 60,000 if tribal and other militia fighters are included. The Saudis reportedly took over as patron when the UAE withdrew its forces in 2019. See Sana'a Center for Strategic Studies, *War's Elusive End—the Yemen Annual Review 2019*, Sana'a, Yemen, 2020; Tom Miles, "Southern Yemenis Warn Exclusion from U.N. Peace Talks Could Trigger New Conflict," Reuters, March 1, 2019.

Drawing on financial and military assistance from the UAE, Al-Zubaidi and Bin Buraik began to forge a new southern movement in 2015, consolidating support from local communities and mobilizing fighters. This movement would begin to challenge the Yemeni government under President Hadi, in pursuit of southern independence. As governor of Aden, Al-Zubaidi used his position to reward loyalists, especially those from his home governorate in Ad-Dhale'a. This would increasingly strain tensions between southerners loyal to Hadi and his interior minister (the "Zomrah camp") and those loyal to Al-Zubaidi (the "Toghma camp"). Tensions mounted in 2016 as Hadi sought to undercut Al-Zubaidi's growing influence by replacing the governor's allies with those loyal to the president.[64]

These disagreements eventually spilled out onto the streets in February 2017, when Hadi's Presidential Guard clashed with UAE-backed forces—loyal to Al-Zubaidi and Bin Buraik—over control of Aden's airport.[65] Although the UAE and Saudi Arabia were able to deescalate the situation, tensions continued to fester. By April 2017, Hadi unceremoniously fired Al-Zubaidi and Bin Buraik.[66]

Following their dismissal, Al-Zubaidi and Bin Buraik announced the formation of the STC on May 11, 2017, assuming the roles of STC president and vice president, respectively. Although still nominally fighting alongside the coalition against the Houthis, the rise of the STC represented a significant, if not irreparable, break from Hadi and his government. This break was more than political. Tensions have resulted in regular, violent clashes for territorial control and targeted assassinations in contested areas.[67]

From the STC's perspective, foremost among its grievances has been the exclusion of southern governorates in ongoing peace negotiations over the civil war with the Houthis. Throughout the conflict, UN peace talks have focused on keeping Yemen unified by first resolving the dispute between the Houthis and the Hadi government.[68] Such a focus has only repeated the mistakes of the past, reinforcing many southerners' perception that they have been politically disenfranchised at the national level. In 2014, the National Dialogue Conference included the "southern question" on its agenda but failed to resolve this issue, in part, because of disagreements within the southern movement, which has long been divided on what exactly the political future of Yemen should look like. Younger activists complained that delegates

---

[64] Since mid-2016 and increasing at the beginning of 2017, our actor-mapping data suggest that the Zomrah camp has been trying to appoint replacements for people affiliated with the governor's Toghma camp and hire more people from the Zomrah camp.

[65] Salisbury, 2018a.

[66] United Nations Human Rights Council, *Annual Report of the United Nations High Commissioner for Human Rights and Reports of the Office of the High Commissioner and the Secretary-General*, Geneva, August 9, 2019.

[67] United Nations Human Rights Council, 2019, p. 12.

[68] Lackner and Al-Hamdani, 2020, p. 2.

representing the southern movement at the National Dialogue Conference, many of whom were appointed by Hadi, were illegitimate and chose instead to boycott the process.[69]

The UN has occasionally enjoyed some success in mediating negotiations between the Houthis and Hadi, but these agreements have not been sustained, in part, because of the exclusion of the STC and other southern leaders. With the STC excluded from participating in the negotiations, key STC leaders, including Al-Zubaidi, warned that they were prepared to spoil the UN process.[70] Although the 2019 Riyadh Agreement and similar efforts have sought to resolve tensions among the Saudi-led coalition, such efforts have often papered over entrenched historical divisions, without resolving any of the underlying problems driving southern separatist dissatisfaction.

Going forward, there are no easy solutions to the "southern problem." But this much is clear: The current strategy of separating these issues from the larger peace process has failed. Southern exclusion is only part of the problem, but it is fixable. Future peace talks should avoid repeating the mistakes of the past and begin to address some of the historical political and economic grievances that underly these tensions.

Shifting Loyalties, Competing Interests, and Divisions Within the South

There have long been competing visions for southern Yemen, which has historically been divided along tribal, regional, and political lines. In the past, these differences led to a "lack of cohesion or strategy among secessionist groups."[71] Although the STC has helped unify some divisions and given voice to historically marginalized groups by amplifying their demands, Al-Zubaidi and Bin Buraik do not speak for all southerners.[72] There may be a shared cause among southerners, but there is no common vision for the future of Yemen.

RAND's actor-mapping data detail the extent to which the STC and UAE have limited reach in such places as Shabwa, where tribal relationships have played just as much, if not more, of a role in determining local influence and control. Initially, the STC tried to win over influential tribal sheikhs in Shabwa, such as Saleh Fareed Bin Mohsen Al-Awlaki, the paramount sheikh of the Al-Awalik tribe, which is the largest tribe in Shabwa and one of the most important in the south (see Figure 4.3). Al-Awlaki enjoys the respect and appreciation of many from his tribe, and he is considered one of the most influential figures in southern Yemen. In 2017, Al-Awlaki joined the STC's leadership body and publicly supported the group's efforts to unify southern

[69] Schmitz, 2014; Salisbury, 2018a; Lackner and Al-Hamdani, 2020, p. 3.

[70] Sana'a Center for Strategic Studies, 2020.

[71] Salisbury, 2018a, p. 1.

[72] Salisbury, 2018a, p. 24.

Yemenis,[73] becoming the group's "chief ally in Shabwa."[74] Al-Awlaki's wide respect within Shabwa, especially for his role as a mediator among local tribes,[75] conferred greater authority and legitimacy on the STC at the time. Yet despite his prominence, most of Al-Awlaki's tribesmen remained supportive of President Hadi and opposed to the STC.

Figure 4.3. Profile of Saleh Fareed Bin Mohsen Al-Awlaki

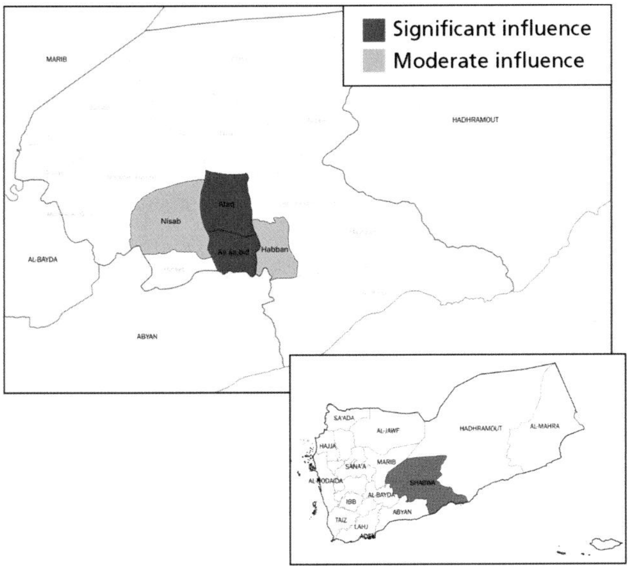

Name: Saleh Fareed Bin Mohsen Al-Awlaki (Arabic: فريد بن محسن العولقي صالح بن)

Current and past positions: Sheikh of the Al-Awalik tribe, member of the Presidium of the STC (2017–2019)

Major areas of influence: Shabwa

Personal history, political allies, and interests: When the Houthi-Saleh alliance entered Shabwa in early 2015, Al-Awlaki led a Shabwa resistance group, which included hundreds of fighters and was very active in the clashes against the Houthis. When the major conflict in Shabwa wound down in August 2015, Al-Awlaki moved to the UAE and participated in all the meetings with Hiraki leadership (i.e., the southern secessionist movement) in the UAE. Reports suggest he has since received support from the UAE.

As local tensions with the STC's leaders grew, Al-Awlaki eventually defected from the group, choosing to pursue an alternative path and a greater flexibility in his political alignments.[76] The specific drivers and timing of Al-Awlaki's break from the STC are not entirely clear. However, the relationship itself was relatively new and represented a historical deviation from the factional politics of southern Yemen. Given the long-standing grievances between Shabwa's Zomrah faction and the Toghma faction that largely compose STC leadership, the relationship was likely a fragile one from the start.

---

[73] Ali Al-Hadayani, "Sheikh Saleh Bin Fared: There Is an International and Regional Understanding for the Need to Form the Southern Transitional Council," Southern Transitional Council, 2018.

[74] Lackner and Al-Hamdani, 2020, p. 24.

[75] Our research with locals described Al-Awlaki as the most prominent sheikh who leads mediation efforts between tribes, works to stop armed conflict, and solves people's problems, especially with the absence of the state in large swathes of the governorate. We discuss these local mediation efforts in greater detail in the next chapter.

[76] Lackner and Al-Hamdani, 2020, p. 24.

This defection would prove consequential for the STC as it began a military offensive in Shabwa in 2019. STC forces were surprised to face significant resistance, given the strength of the local Shabwa Elite Forces that had supported the UAE in a previous campaign to eradicate Al-Qaeda in the Arabian Peninsula (AQAP) in the governorate. Despite the UAE's influence in the governorate, "prominent Shabwa tribes—including some members of the Shabwa Elite Forces—declined to join the fight against government forces," including Al-Awlaki.[77] Force cohesion suffered when different tribes supported opposing sides, dividing units.[78] The STC's eventual defeat in Shabwa, which resulted in the redeployment of the Shabwa Elite Forces to Aden, proved to be a stark "reality check for the group," and it showed Al-Zubaidi's vision of southern Yemen united under the STC banner to be "fanciful."[79]

This defeat would not be the last setback for the STC. The group has also faced resistance in Hadramawt, which may represent an altogether thornier challenge to the viability of a future "south Yemen." Much of this resistance has to do with economic interests. Although most of southern Yemen has historically suffered, some areas have fared better than others during the recent conflict. Hadramawt is one such case. In the past, the governorate's oil wealth had not "directly benefited Hadhramis, causing some resentment."[80] But Hadramawt's leaders have exploited the political vacuum to expand the governorate's local autonomy in the midst of civil war, and they are not likely to favor returning to the status quo ante.[81] These leaders have grown this influence by assiduously staying neutral as they "advocate for local Hadhrami concerns," such as keeping a greater share of their oil wealth.[82]

One such figure is Governor Faraj Salmeen Al-Bahsani, who also commands the Second Military Region (see Figure 4.4). By all accounts, Al-Bahsani is principally loyal to Hadhrami interests, having navigated the Hadi and STC dispute without taking a clear side.[83] He maintains good relations with Saudi Arabia and the UAE alike, both of which have economic and strategic interests in Hadramawt's coast and port access.[84]

Like its neighbor Shabwa, Hadramawt is often overlooked in peace talks, but its importance is undeniable. Together, these governorates span nearly half of Yemen's land mass and contain a disproportionate share of the country's oil fields. Their territories also provide vital access to the coast, which is critical to pipelines for gas export and other commerce.[85] But perhaps most

---

77 Sana'a Center for Strategic Studies, 2020.

78 Sana'a Center for Strategic Studies, 2020.

79 Sana'a Center for Strategic Studies, 2020.

80 Lackner and Al-Hamdani, 2020, p. 15.

81 Sana'a Center for Strategic Studies, 2020.

82 Lackner and Al-Hamdani, 2020, p. 18.

83 Lackner and Al-Hamdani, 2020, p. 17.

84 Lackner and Al-Hamdani, 2020, p. 18.

85 Salisbury, 2018a, p. 19.

importantly, these governorates have historically served as the base for AQAP and other jihadist groups. Ignoring these areas, excluding their leaders, and leaving the grievances unaddressed are a recipe for future instability.

Figure 4.4. Profile of Faraj Salmeen Al-Bahsani

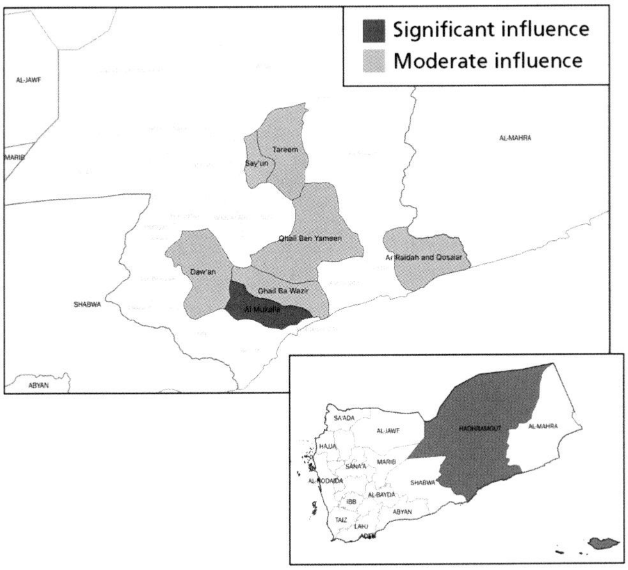

Name: Faraj Salmeen Al-Bahsani (Arabic: فرج سالمين البحساني)

Current and past positions: Governor of Hadramawt (2017–present), Commander of the Second Military Region (2015–present)

Major areas of influence: Hadramawt

Personal history, political allies, and interests: Al-Bahsani's position as governor gives him authority in the whole governorate, but his real power is concentrated in Sahel Hadramawt. He has remained silent on controversial issues related to Emirati activities in Mukalla, especially the targeting of Islahi activists and party officials. Al-Bahsani is technically and symbolically the head of the Elite Forces in his capacity as commander of the Second Military Region, but decisions regarding the Elite Forces are not actually in his hands.

Actor Mapping and Lessons for Peacebuilding

Interpersonal rivalries and conflicts have certainly contributed to the divisions that have nearly destroyed the Saudi-led coalition, but the underlying cause remains the historical grievances that many southerners feel remain unaddressed. Figure 4.5 shows a stylized network model, mapping the relationships between some of the key actors we identified in our analysis. These actors, their grievances, and the complex interactions between them will drive the success of any future peace talks and any effort to build enduring peace.

Among the actors we profiled, Al-Zubaidi (actor 1) has the most connections. His network is built on long-standing political relationships with southern secessionists, who are concentrated in Ad-Dhale'a but also reach into Aden, Shabwa, and Hadramawt. Bin Buraik (actor 2) complements Al-Zubaidi by leveraging a network that is smaller, but it extends relationships to actors outside the core STC areas, including in Taiz. Notably, Bin Buraik's ties are exclusively based on his relationships with other militant Salafis. Together, their networks span across southern governorates and include a diverse mix of communities. Although this influence may not be sufficient to unite southern Yemenis under the STC banner, it is enough to derail the peace process if they continue to be excluded. Incorporating these actors, and better addressing their grievances, may be essential to peace.

Figure 4.5. Elite Networks in Southern Yemen

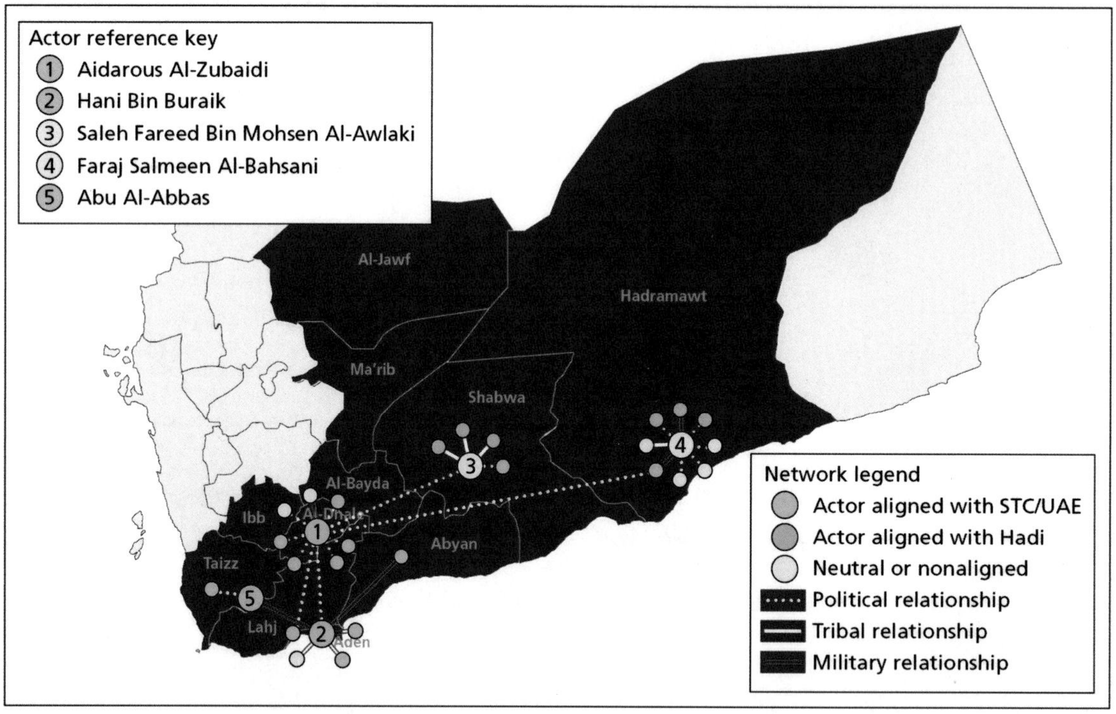

SOURCE: RAND actor-mapping data, 2017.

Sustaining such a peace, however, will depend on winning over other key actors with different motivations. In Shabwa, this coalition must include prominent tribal sheikhs, such as Saleh Al-Awlaki (actor 3), who has ties to the STC but has forged an alternative path in the midst of chaos and coalition infighting. Al-Awlaki's network is built on cross-cutting tribal ties, which include some actors who support Hadi and others who support the STC. These relationships offer a flexibility and an advantage in mediating between the two camps.

Prominent figures in Hadramawt, such as Governor Al-Bahsani (actor 4), have also struck a careful balance navigating between the STC and Hadi while carving out greater local autonomy and pursuing Hadramawt's economic interests. Such influential actors speak with authority within their communities, making it imperative that they buy into the peace process. Al-Bahsani's large network includes Hadi, STC, and nonaligned actors, and his relationships are built on a mix of political, tribal, and military ties. But whereas Al-Awlaki has a direct connection to Al-Zubaidi through his past membership in the STC, Al-Bahsani's ties are more indirect, through a third party. Such actors are often seen as relatively marginal in the big picture, but including them in the peace process may be critical to rebuilding trust and bridging the divide within the coalition.

But there must be limits to inclusion. Not all actors can be accommodated, nor does every warlord or Salafi commander deserve a seat at the table, even if they can mobilize fighters. For potential spoilers, such as Abu Al-Abbas in Taiz (see Figure 4.6), having power is not sufficient. Al-Abbas (actor 5) is a militant Salafi commander who has become notorious for his ties to AQAP and his forces' bloody clashes with allied Islamists in Taiz. During the war, Al-Abbas has grown his local influence while drawing on Emirati support. The UAE has been willing to overlook Al-Abbas's unsavory ties because they share an enemy in common: Yemen's Al-Islah party, which is an offshoot of the Muslim Brotherhood.[86]

Figure 4.6. Profile of Abu Al-Abbas

Name: Abu Al-Abbas (Arabic: ابو العباس)

Current and past positions: Commander of the Abu Al-Abbas Battalions, Salafi sheikh

Major areas of influence: Taizz

Personal history, political allies, and interests: Abu Al-Abbas became the coalition's point of contact for Salafi resistance fighters in Taizz in March 2015. The UAE has since become his major patron. This material support, however, is more limited in comparison to the UAE's support for Salafi resistance fighters in Aden. During the conflict, Al-Abbas has significantly increased his influence, having become the most powerful Salafi commander in Taizz. His fighters control parts of Taizz and collect taxes from local businesses while also performing some administrative duties.

For such figures, the status quo may preferable (and more profitable) than peace. Those who benefit from war, using conflict to amass wealth and expand their power, have little interest in peace. If given a place at the bargaining table, such actors are more likely to spoil the negotiations than contribute to a peace agreement. How these actors' malign influence can be mitigated (e.g., selective incentives for complying with a peace agreement) is an open and contested question—but one that must be answered if peace is to endure. Notably, Al-Abbas's network appears relatively limited in Taiz, and our research suggests that his support on the ground may be somewhat exaggerated.

This account is by no means intended to be exhaustive. Every governorate entails its own distinct challenges, arrayed across a range of key actors and local leaders. To fully document their historical grievances would be a monumental analytic task. Although this chapter focused on key actors in Yemen's southern governorates, similar themes of political disenfranchisement and economic marginalization have driven conflict in the north. Such historical grievances also contributed to the rise of the Houthi movement.[87] Ultimately, our analysis suggests that the peace

---

[86] Daniel Byman, "Saudi Arabia and the United Arab Emirates Have a Disastrous Yemen Strategy," Brookings Institution, July 17, 2018.

[87] See Chapter Three in Salmoni, Loidolt, and Wells, 2010.

process must engage local actors across the country in an inclusive fashion, affording opportunities to address underlying grievances that have underpinned the conflict to date.

UN-mediated negotiations will be critical to securing a peace agreement, but they are not themselves sufficient. Before, during, and after these negotiations, Yemeni elites from across the country will have to do the hard work underlying reconciliation. Such work will depend on key local actors, such as Al-Awlaki and Al-Bahsani, whose broad respect, deep community ties, and pragmatic leadership will be critical throughout the long, slow, and difficult peace process. Some figures, such as Abu Al-Abbas, are likely irreconcilable, but others may be co-opted given the proper incentives. Most importantly, Al-Zubaidi and Bin Buraik could be swayed if guaranteed a sufficient stake in Yemen's future. If not, they will look to spoil the peace process. The next chapter describes some of the challenges to come in sustaining such a process at the local level.

5. Local Conflict Drivers and Mediation Practices: Challenges to an Enduring Peace

After more than five years of civil war—and before that, decades of political disenfranchisement and economic marginalization—many Yemenis distrust the central government and will look skeptically at any elite pact that ends the conflict with a unified state. Given this pervasive distrust, a peace agreement negotiated among elites is not enough to ensure an enduring peace in Yemen. For sustainable peace to become a reality, it must take root among the communities, tribes, and institutions that make up Yemen's rich social fabric. Such a peace must be built and sustained at the local level, which will require local mediators whose positions of authority and influence within their communities provide legitimacy that faraway elites in a remote capitol do not enjoy.

To inform future peacebuilding and peacekeeping efforts, RAND's research mapped local drivers of conflict and captured lessons about the most-common and most-effective mediation mechanisms that could contribute to community resiliency and peacekeeping. Using detailed on-the-ground interviews conducted by our Yemeni partners with community leaders in 11 governorates across Yemen, RAND built a data set of more than 400 conflict episodes to better understand the causes, consequences, and key actors involved in the escalation and mediation of local conflicts. In each interview, our Yemeni partners asked these community leaders to discuss at least one conflict that had been resolved and one that had not,[88] as well as to provide a narrative description of the factors that led to the resolution or continuation of each conflict. This research expands on prior RAND work in Yemen, where we fielded a nationally representative survey to understand the local drivers of support for political violence.[89]

Although much attention has been given to the international nature of the conflict, and the intransigence of the two major Yemeni factions, our research suggests that many drivers of conflict are actually local in nature, based on economic grievances rooted in structural inequities. There are any number of factors that may drive conflict at the local level, but the single most common driver is competition for land and other resources. In more rural areas, such as Shabwa and Hadramawt, these conflicts often derive from tribal clashes over territory with valuable resources (e.g., oil, water). In urban spaces, such as Aden and Taiz, these conflicts tend to be neighborhood disputes over contested property lines. At a deeper level, all of these conflicts,

[88] Whether or not a conflict was assessed as "resolved" was left to the judgment of the interviewee. In the 220 interviews conducted for this research, with 20 interviews conducted in each of the 11 governorates, 190 interviewees were able to provide examples both a resolved and unresolved conflict.

[89] Eric Robinson, P. Kathleen Frier, Kim Cragin, Melissa A. Bradley, Daniel Egel, Bryce Loidolt, and Paul S. Steinberg, *What Factors Cause Individuals to Reject Violent Extremism in Yemen?* Santa Monica, Calif.: RAND Corporation, RR-1727-OSD, 2017.

however ordinary they may seem, are rooted in a long history of insecure and contested property rights. This history traces its origins back decades, when southerners repeatedly suffered from property seizures and land expropriation.

But our research also highlights how Yemen's rich tradition of local, informal mediation has persisted throughout the conflict. Tribal sheiks, community leaders, and other local actors play an essential role in conflict mediation across Yemen and will likely be critical to sustaining the eventual peace agreement. In this chapter, we describe how local context and history often shape the relationship between state and nonstate actors. Unsurprisingly, our analysis revealed that formal government-led efforts to mediate conflict were few and far between—and ineffective when they did occur. In some cases, informal mediators substituted for the state, while at other times they complemented state authorities. Ultimately, neither type of mediator is sufficient on its own to sustain a peace agreement—an enduring peace will depend on leveraging local, informal mediators in the short term while the state slowly builds its capacity and earns the trust of local communities.

Land Rights, Natural Resources, and Conflict in Yemen

Drawing on hundreds of interviews with military, government, community, and tribal actors across Yemen, we find that local conflict tends to be driven by routine disputes involving basic resources and interpersonal disagreements. Disputes over land are the single most common driver of local conflict in our data, mirroring the result found by historical analyses of conflict in Yemen.[90]

For decades, land disputes have been a regular source of local conflict in Yemen, particularly in the south. Dating back to 1967, property seizures and redistributions became so commonplace in Aden and elsewhere that multiple "legitimate" claims developed to ownership of property often developed.[91] In 2013, President Hadi empaneled a committee of judges to solve land-related disputes as a confidence-building measure on the eve of the National Dialogue Conference.[92] But these efforts proved largely unsuccessful, in part because competing claims were difficult to adjudicate, and the Yemeni government lacked the financial means to provide restitution to those whose claims were unsuccessful.

Most land disputes are territorial in nature (see Figure 5.1). We define *territorial disputes* as conflicts over some contested area of ambiguous ownership (e.g., a road or market). These conflicts typically involve clashes between tribes and other groups who claim control or

---

[90] E.g., National Democratic Institute, *Yemen: Tribal Conflict Management Program Research Report*, Washington, D.C., 2007.

[91] We thank Ambassador Gerald M. Feierstein for this helpful insight, highlighting the unique difficulties of resolving land disputes in southern Yemen using failed previous efforts to redistribute land.

[92] Jens Kambeck, "Land Disputes in Yemen," in Helen Lackner, ed., *Why Yemen Matters: A Society in Transition*, London: Saqi Books, 2014.

authority over some broadly defined area. By contrast, residential disputes are less common and tend to involve well-defined property lines, neighborhood disagreements, and disputes over residential structures (e.g., squatters' rights).

Figure 5.1. The Source of Land Disputes

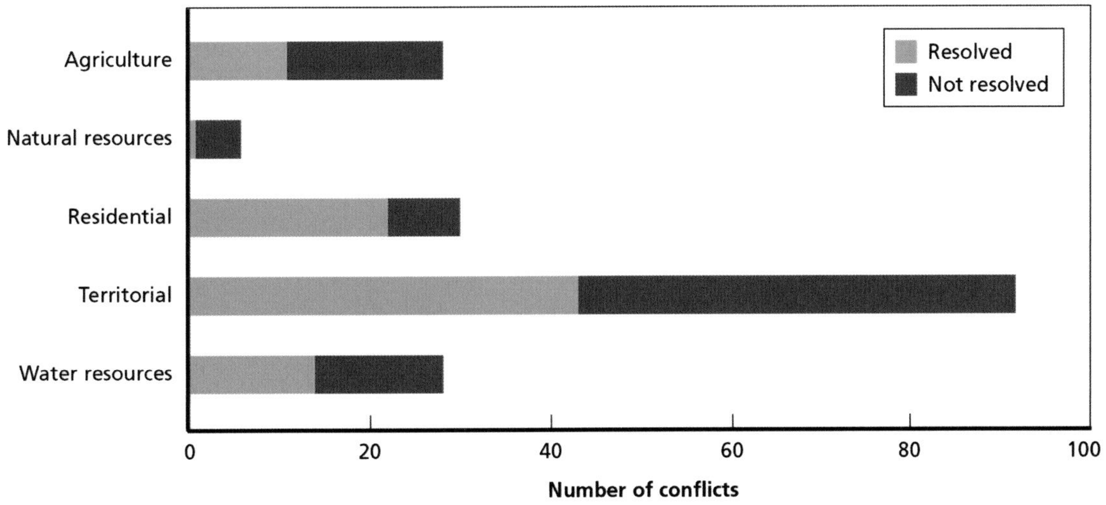

SOURCE: RAND conflict drivers data, 2017.

Many of these territorial disputes occur in more-rural governorates, where tribes play a major role (e.g., Al-Bayda, Al-Jawf). One such dispute arose in Marib in 2015, when a tribe began constructing a road in an area of contested ownership. A neighboring tribe demanded that the road be demolished, but this call went unmet and the tribes began a series of violent clashes that left six dead. As the interviewee noted, "the borders between tribes in Yemen are prickly," and this new road inflamed border tensions. Eventually, a third tribe was able to broker a cease-fire, but this effort ultimately failed. As neither tribe would concede, fighting resumed and the conflict remained unresolved.

Although territorial disputes were slightly more likely to go unresolved than not in our analysis, resource-based conflicts often posed greater challenges. After decades of war and chronic underinvestment, Yemen remains woefully undeveloped, with few commercial opportunities, making valuable natural resources an attractive but scarce revenue stream. Arable land that is suited to the cultivation of qat is also valuable and drives many agricultural land disputes. Like other precious resources, these agricultural disputes can be difficult to mediate when the land is especially valuable.

Land disputes involving natural resources were particularly common in Shabwah. Of these natural resource conflicts, three disputes centered on land with lucrative gas pipelines, which make them especially valuable for potential "compensation and work," according to an interviewee. One such case can be seen in Shabwah's Jardan district, where two neighboring tribes disputed ownership of land with a liquefied natural gas pipeline. The conflict initially escalated when one tribe destroyed vehicles owned by the other. Unlike most resource conflicts, however, this case involved an intervention by third-party tribal sheikhs who were able to successfully mediate the dispute.

By contrast, residential disputes were often much easier to resolve. These disputes tended to occur in urban areas and derived from confusion over neighbors' property lines or public-private land-use disagreements (such as sewage or road access). Ownership and property lines were often clear in these cases, relieving mediators from having to sort through complicated claims. Instead, mediation in residential disputes tended to be fairly simple and focused on calming tensions and soothing grievances among neighbors. In other cases, disputes arose from illegal squatters. Typically, these disputes involved unemployed or homeless youth seizing some home or other property that was temporarily vacant.

Absence of Formal Mediation Mechanisms

In addition to the drivers of local conflict, our interviews also explored the sources of mediation in each governorate, identifying the formal and informal actors who play a role in local conflict resolution. Across nearly all of the governorates analyzed in our research, the weakness or sheer absence of formal governing institutions has allowed ordinary grievances to escalate into conflict, and left many local conflicts to be resolved informally.

In Aden, for example, our research identified multiple instances in which the lack of a formal judicial process allowed armed groups to justify the seizure of property for their own use in otherwise peaceful areas and individual citizens to loot in the absence of effective policing. Criminal courts in Aden were almost universally derided as ineffective, with interviewees describing the courts as "weak" or "completely absent," and the officials staffing them were allegedly "afraid to leave their houses."

Similarly, many of those interviewed in Ad-Dhale'a perceived formal systems, such as state authorities or the courts, to be corrupt, and our research identified that formal authorities were not able to resolve any of the conflicts in which they intervened. Shabwah's state authorities had a comparably poor record, intervening in only three conflicts and failing to resolve each case. State authority and formal mediation were also weak in contested areas, such as Al-Jawf. In Taiz, formal authorities played a noticeably larger role in attempting to resolve conflicts than other governorates. But these institutions still suffered from the poor reputation and imperfect track record seen throughout the rest of Yemen. Of the five episodes in our data in which formal authorities in Taiz served as the sole mediator of a conflict, not a single one was resolved.

Yemenis' lack of trust in formal institutions to resolve conflict will prove a significant impediment to sustaining peace, in the event an agreement can be reached among the civil war's major factions. Fortunately, Yemen's rich history of informal mediation by community and tribal leaders has stepped in to fill the void.

Informal Conflict Resolution During Civil War

Yemen's local mediators tend to fall into one of three categories: state or government authorities, community leaders, and tribal sheikhs. Where state or government authorities have been absent, Yemen's long, rich history of tribal and community-based mediation has stepped in to fill the void.[93] Although many tribal sheikhs and other leaders hold significant respect within their communities—often, more respect than government officials—these roles fall outside the formal state domain. With the national conflict's onset and near collapse of the state, it is important to understand the conditions under which these informal actors compete with, complement, or simply replace formal institutions.

The local and historical context shapes the relationship between formal and informal conflict mediators in each governorate. These relationships vary in important ways and often determine the process through which conflict is mediated, effectively or otherwise. This variation can partly be seen in Figure 5.2, which plots the likelihood of conflict resolution according to the types of mediators involved. Tribal sheikhs and community leaders were not only more likely to intervene but also more likely to successfully resolve a dispute than not. By contrast, state authorities intervened less often and tend to be less successful.

Figure 5.2. Distribution of Mediators

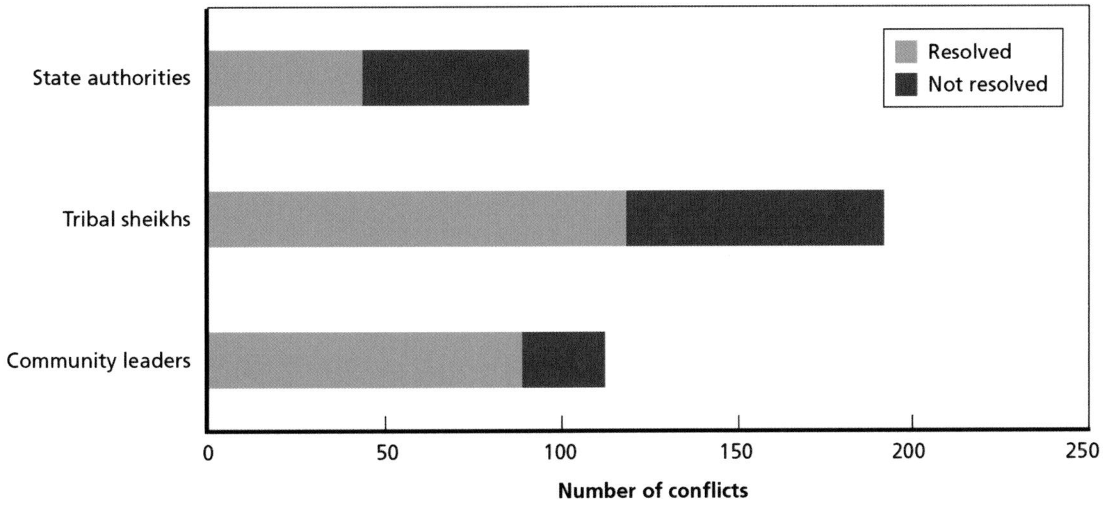

SOURCE: RAND conflict drivers data, 2017.

In some cases, the absence of functioning state authorities (e.g., in remote rural areas) made informal mediation a necessity. But in others, the lack of formal mediation cannot be explained by state weakness alone. In the midst of the conflict, Marib became one of the most effective

[93] Erica Gaston and Nadwa al-Dawsari, *Dispute Resolution and Justice Provision in Yemen's Transition*, Washington, D.C.: United States Institute of Peace, 2014; Nadwa al-Dawsari, "Tribal Governance and Stability in Yemen," Carnegie Endowment for International Peace, April 24, 2012.

governorate authorities, with its leader, Sultan Al-Arada, growing his power and influence. At the same time, however, Marib has maintained its traditions and still relies heavily on tribal mediation, often as a substitute for state-led mediation. A similar dynamic can be seen in Hadramawt, where local authorities have carved out greater autonomy in the midst of civil war.[94] But as in Marib, tribal actors continue to play a vital, complementary role to the state.

In these examples, like similar cases found in other governorates, formal and informal mediators represent substitutes. A tribal sheikh may adjudicate the same types of disputes that are found in the local court system, offering potential options to local communities. Under such conditions, informal actors may even compete with formal state actors. In other, more-developed countries, such extralegal competition is often seen as a dangerous encroachment on state authority and may even portend future challenges. But in many Yemeni governorates, the fractured state and dysfunctional judicial system has made informal conflict mediators a necessity.

To some degree, these examples all position formal and informal mediators as distinct or even antagonistic substitutes. But in other cases, these actors may complement each other, working in tandem to arbitrate a dispute. In Hadramawt, formal and informal mediation processes interact in especially complex and complementary ways. Tribal sheikhs and community leaders frequently partner with state authorities at various stages of the conflict mediation process, hinting at the governorate's prewar history of a relatively capable judicial system.[95] In some cases identified in our analysis, this process can include multiple rounds of mediation efforts, with a repeated interaction between informal mediators and the courts. State authorities also provided police reports and records of past events, or deployed security forces to end a violent confrontation, allowing local mediation to begin in earnest. Such formal-informal complementarity helped to resolve five conflicts in Hadramawt captured in our data.

But in some cases, informal actors can actually escalate conflict rather than defuse it. Such escalation has been particularly common in Ibb, where political parties have intervened, only to polarize the conflict. In 2015, a personal dispute between two men escalated when one killed the other, drawing in their respective tribes. One tribe had ties to the General People's Congress and the other to Islah; therefore, the tribal sheikhs who intervened were viewed with skepticism and distrust because of their political associations. Instead of resolving the dispute, local reports suggested that the mediators' intervention just escalated the conflict by unnecessarily entangling the tribes and their copartisans.

Whether tribal sheikhs or concerned civil society leaders, mediators are most effective when they are embedded in the local community and appreciate its history and complex relationships. The importance of this local embeddedness can be seen in a conflict from Taiz, where family

---

[94] Badr Basalmah, *Local Governance in Yemen: Challenges and Opportunities*, Berlin: Berghof Foundation, May 2018.

[95] Gaston and al-Dawsari, 2014, p. 9.

members began to build a path from the main road to their house, partially infringing on their neighbor's property. Initially, "most of those who intervened in the conflict were nonresidents of the region and did not know" the area well, according to an interviewee. These efforts failed. Eventually, a mediator with good relations with both families intervened. This local mediator was able to convince the family building the road to cover the costs of construction and maintenance while allowing others to also access the road. In the absence of formal institutions to address these disputes, local mediators can step in.

How Local Conflict Can Threaten National Peace

Ignoring local conflict dynamics and marginalizing local stakeholders could jeopardize efforts to realize an enduring peace in Yemen as part of future peacebuilding efforts. There must be "local ownership" throughout the process, from negotiating peace to postconflict stabilization.[96] After all, "any peace process not embraced by those who have to live with it is likely to fail."[97]

Sustaining the peace will depend on incentivizing local actors who have sufficient authority and popular legitimacy in their communities to intervene and mediate disputes before they escalate. Our research shows how local conflicts that arise from straightforward disputes can quickly entangle tribes, political parties, and militant groups. Interpersonal disputes often draw in other groups or actors, especially in the absence of functional state authorities, which is all too common in Yemen. These outside actors can play the role of mediator or provocateur—and which they decide may determine whether fragile peace can be built and sustained.

Either way, any effort to leverage formal state institutions in Yemen for peacebuilding must harness the constructive potential of informal local mediation, or the effort will be doomed to failure. At a minimum, peacebuilding efforts must ensure that informal local mediation continues unabated while formal government-led mediation processes are given time to develop, mature, and be seen as legitimate by the Yemeni communities they are meant to support.

---

[96] Timothy Donais, "Empowerment or Imposition? Dilemmas of Local Ownership in Post-Conflict Peacebuilding Processes," *Peace and Change*, Vol. 34, No. 1, 2009, p. 3.

[97] Donais, 2009, p. 3.

6. A Framework for Building an Enduring Peace

In this final chapter, we provide the contours of a framework for building an enduring peace in Yemen. This process may take decades. Yemenis cannot afford to rush the process of rebuilding (or establishing anew) the political, economic, and security institutions necessary to sustain peace. Recognizing this challenge, our framework is built on a phased approach, focusing on Yemen's most-immediate needs while working in parallel to address the political and economic inequities that have long troubled its citizens.

We see two possible pathways forward for Yemen. The first pathway is to continue with and double down on the current efforts that focus on national reconciliation. These efforts have been led by the UN and appear to enjoy broad support within the international community, which has worked to preserve Yemen's sovereignty and geographic integrity. This pathway to national reconciliation has focused on first brokering an agreement with the Houthis to end the war before moving on to resolving regional or local grievances.

The second pathway would be to refocus international peacebuilding and state-building efforts on Yemen's southern and eastern governorates, at least in the near term. With battle lines largely frozen and competing sides dug in, there has been little progress in these regions through diplomacy. The territory currently controlled by the government of Yemen and its affiliated forces constitutes—approximately—three of the six federal regions agreed to in the National Dialogue Conference.[98] Along this second pathway, efforts could focus on stabilizing these three regions as part of a longer-term project of reconciliation built around a national, federated government.

Our phased approach is designed to be flexible to either of these pathways, although each offers substantial challenges. The primary challenge to the first pathway is the widening gap in bargaining positions between the Houthis and the multitude of other political actors on the coalition side of the conflict. The second pathway will require security commitments from the international community to ensure the integrity of the regions and contain competition within the coalition, as well as a willingness to accept a divided Yemen over at least the medium term. Regardless, both pathways will require patience from the Yemeni people and a robust and enduring commitment from the international community.

[98] Tobias Thiel, "Yemen's Imposed Federal Boundaries," Middle East Research and Information Project, July 20, 2015.

A Phased Approach to Peace

An enduring end to the conflict will require a phased approach that provides political resolution and economic stabilization while guaranteeing the security of citizens across Yemen's political and social strata. Figure 6.1 summarizes the major lines of effort required to achieve this peace. Broadly defined, there are two related lines of effort: political reconciliation and institutional capacity (the blue shading) and economic reform and service provision (the green shading). This figure maps out how these efforts evolve across three phases, from stabilization and relief in the near term, to a transitional period of institution building in the medium term, culminating in democratic consolidation and sustained development over the long term. None of these phases is fixed and will undoubtedly require adaptation and flexibility over time, but they each depend on key milestones (the arrows) being met if Yemen is to achieve an enduring peace.

Figure 6.1. A Phased Approach to Building an Enduring Peace

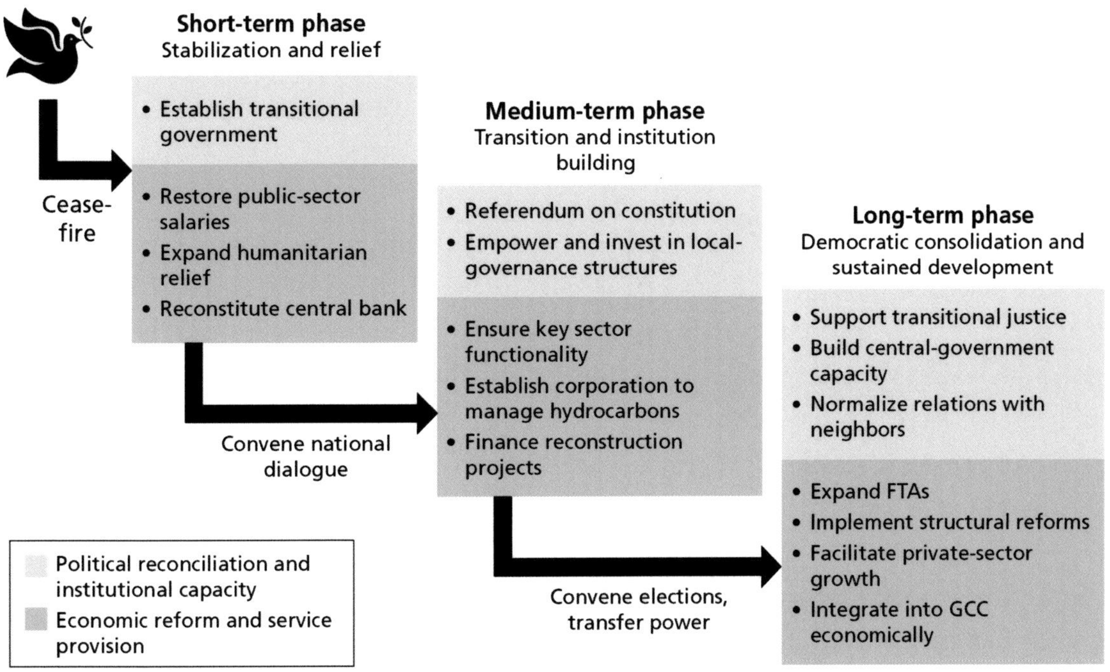

SOURCE: RAND analysis based on interviews with senior U.S. officials, UN representatives, Yemeni civil society leaders, academics, and international diplomats from across Europe and the Middle East, 2019–2020.
NOTE: FTA = free-trade agreement; GCC = Gulf Cooperation Council.

Stabilization and Relief

In the near term, Yemen's most immediate challenge is clear: Negotiate a cease-fire and open up the country to provide urgent humanitarian relief. This process will be challenging, as recent events both in the north (e.g., Houthi offensives in Al-Jawf and Marib) and south (e.g., intracoalition clashes for control over Socotra) have revealed little interest in peace among the parties. And, here, the international community will have to decide which pathway to follow, either remaining focused on broad national reconciliation or pivoting toward state building in the southern and eastern regions of a divided Yemen. A negotiated cease-fire for the second pathway could be built around the former Riyadh agreement. Although this agreement ultimately failed, it offered a framework for building a coalition between Hadi's government and Al-Zubaidi's STC. For the first pathway to succeed, a negotiated cease-fire and a reconciliation between Hadi and Al-Zubaidi are likely preconditions before any national cease-fire could be seriously contemplated.[99]

After securing a broad cease-fire, the international community must work to quickly expand humanitarian relief. These efforts will crucially depend on the support and compliance of local and regional actors. One important step is disbursing public-sector salaries across the entire country, which will inject much-needed capital while helping to restore essential services. For the national reconciliation pathway to succeed, the coalition will have to end its blockade and allow for an expansion of humanitarian relief and assistance. If given a chance, this phase should culminate in two critical milestones: reconstituting the Central Bank of Yemen and establishing an inclusive transitional government that represents actors from across Yemen's political spectrum.[100] Moreover, Yemen's dilapidated health infrastructure will require immediate international support and investments in local health care capacity.

Transition and Institution Building

With a transitional government in place, Yemenis can begin the long, hard process of political and economic institution building, in an effort to redress the underlying political and economic inequalities discussed throughout this report. During this phase, a transitional government will have two immediate tasks: (1) Build an inclusive framework for a new national dialogue process and (2) ensure that critical sectors are functional and can provide services. Both of these tasks will depend on the support of the international community, which will need to provide assistance and help mediate disputes during these early but critical steps.

This process must address the historical disenfranchisement and structural inequities that underly conflict in Yemen. It must also provide meaningful representation to the myriad groups that have historically been excluded in Yemen. Such an inclusive process is necessary to address

---

[99] On the Houthi side, although there is far more unity and a clear command and control flowing down from Abdul Malik al-Houthi, conditions on the ground make peace less attractive. Given their recent gains in the offensives in Al-Jawf and Marib, the Houthis do not appear inclined to peace at present. Bringing them back to the table will likely depend on the Houthis suffering a major defeat on the battlefield or assurances that, were they to make peace, the offer would include control over key ministries or resources.

[100] The collapse of the central bank in 2016 has led to a disastrous competition over monetary control and precipitated a currency crisis. This crisis, and its effects on everyday Yemenis, exemplifies the conflict and how its costs can reverberate throughout the country. For more on this topic, see Anthony Biswell, *Yemen Economic Bulletin: The War for Monetary Control Enters a Dangerous New Phase*, Sana'a, Yemen: Sana'a Center for Strategic Studies, January 21, 2020.

the complex interests of different groups and actors involved in the conflict, many of whom have gained influence during the civil war, but also to redress the underlying local grievances that drive Yemen's historical instability.

Through this dialogue, Yemenis will have to decide how to resolve these grievances and begin to rebuild the state. Yemen's political institutions are broken, offering Yemenis an opportunity to craft a new, more inclusive political system. Such a system should expand opportunities for meaningful political participation and empower governance structures at the local and regional level. During the conflict, pockets of subnational governance have flourished in such places as Marib and Hadramawt, revealing an underlying resilience within local communities. It will take years, if not decades, to rebuild the central government's institutional capacity. In the meantime, Yemenis and the international community should invest in and further empower subnational structures capable of addressing local and regional grievances. Yemen's rich history of informal mediation provides a useful starting point to build effective governance at the local level, allowing the state to gradually build its capacity and earn the trust of local communities.

Achieving an enduring peace will also depend on rebuilding Yemen's economic institutions. During this transitional period, Yemenis and the international community face a daunting task: to develop the institutions and infrastructure to ensure that basic services and assistance are provided to citizens in great need, while also setting the foundation for long-term stability and development. This political transition may offer opportunities that have been politically infeasible in the past, as a transformation of Yemen's economy will likely require a major restructuring of how Yemen manages its hydrocarbon resources, the development of a functional land registration system that addresses historical grievances, and an enforceable system for managing water resources.[101]

Democratic Consolidation and Sustained Development

The final and most nebulous phase in Yemen's path toward an enduring peace begins with the first postconflict elections and a peaceful transfer of power from the transitional government. This new and legitimate government will need to continue the efforts begun in earlier periods, focusing on building democratic institutions and norms while pursuing structural reforms critical to long-term economic growth.

By this period, Yemen's de jure political institutions should already be well established and ratified by popular referendum. But these formal institutions are not sufficient to ensure political stability or even democratic survival. To succeed, a democracy must slowly consolidate around a set of shared norms that help regulate political competition and contestation. For postconflict states, developing these norms often depends on transitional justice efforts that can help a society

---

[101] See, for example, World Bank, *The Republic of Yemen: Unlocking the Potential for Economic Growth*, Washington, D.C., October 2015.

reconcile with its past and begin to heal its collective trauma. As Yemenis wrestle with this process of justice and reconciliation, the central government will have to continue growing its institutional capacity to take on greater responsibility. Over time, the Yemeni state must become more capable and self-reliant. Once no longer dependent on external support from rich Persian Gulf States, Yemen should be able to pursue normal relations with its neighbors.

Yemen's economic needs go far beyond its immediate humanitarian requirements. As our research lays bare, much of the conflict has been driven by structural inequities separating south from north, elites from ordinary citizens, and haves from have-nots. Facilitating private-sector-led growth, managing Yemen's natural resources, and leveraging Yemen's strategic location for the benefit of all Yemenis will require unprecedented public-private coordination and leadership. In this, there will be the need for financial, technical, and political support from the international community and a commitment to sustain this support for at least a decade, if not decades.

More importantly, Yemen's internal political differences must not be allowed to sabotage the economic reconstruction of the country. Satisfying immediate humanitarian requirements while creating employment opportunities for all Yemenis willing and able to work will do much to address the economic disenfranchisement underlying the current conflict—but only if key actors and local constituencies believe that their long-standing grievances are not better addressed through continued violence. On the whole, this phased approach must be Yemeni-led to succeed, but it will also require coordinated and sustained commitment from the international community.

Management and Coordination: The Role of the International Community

Although the foundations of an enduring peace must be Yemeni, there is much that the international community can and should do to support this process. First and foremost, international actors must recognize that the pursuit of their own political, economic, and security interests cannot come at the expense of peace in Yemen. The current system, in which regional and global actors seek opportunistic partnerships to further their parochial objectives, has perpetuated the conflict and made reconciliation more difficult at both the local and the national level. From Saudi competition for influence in eastern Yemen,[102] to Emirati commercial and maritime interests along the southern coast,[103] to Iranian machinations in Houthi-controlled areas of northern Yemen,[104] no actor is without blame. But the international community cannot afford to let regional interests and competition continue to derail a peace process that should foremost address underlying Yemeni grievances.

---

[102] Ahmed Nagi, "Mahra, Yemen: A Shadow Conflict Worth Watching," Carnegie Middle East Center, 2020; Brian Perkins, "Saudi Arabia and the UAE in al-Mahra: Securing Interests, Disrupting Local Order, and Shaping a Southern Military," *Terrorism Monitor* (Jamestown Foundation), March 1, 2019.

[103] Eleonora Ardemagni, "The UAE's Security-Economic Nexus in Yemen," Carnegie Endowment for International Peace, July 19, 2018.

[104] Johnston et al., 2020.

No single power has the capacity to unilaterally dictate the terms for peace, making it critical that the international community come together and commit to a coordinated approach to Yemen's security. This approach should be consistent and emphasize the mutual interests in a stable and peaceful Yemen. In recent months, even Iran has indicated that it is more willing to support the negotiations and contribute to the peace process, lest it be marginalized in any deal that the Houthis make with its rival Saudi Arabia.[105] Such progress should be welcomed and encouraged as the international community builds a broad framework for the peace process.

With such an inclusive framework in place, the international community must be willing to make an unprecedented commitment to peace, establishing an international body that has both the mission and the resources to oversee and support what will be a decades-long process of reconciliation, reconstruction, and redevelopment. Structurally, this international body may take any number of forms, but it must have the authority of an empowered UN mission and include the major international stakeholders and donor states from the Gulf. Many of these actors will be critical to managing and financing the postconflict mission, making it imperative that they have a voice in shaping these efforts.

Although these international actors deserve a voice, they cannot dictate terms to the people of Yemen. For this process to succeed, this international body must enjoy popular legitimacy within Yemen—and to do that it has to be Yemeni-led. And just as a transitional Yemeni government requires broad inclusion, so too should this body, providing a voice to different political actors from across Yemen.

Combined, the steps needed to secure an enduring peace in Yemen represent a tall order. Our work suggests ways in which progress can be made, however, and offers glimmers of hope for a better future.

---

[105] Samuel Ramani, "Iran's Post-Conflict Vision in Yemen," Carnegie Endowment for International Peace, December 11, 2019.

References

Aboudi, Sami, “Allies of Yemen Houthis Seize Aden Airport, Close In on President,” Reuters, March 25, 2015. As of July 21, 2020: https://uk.reuters.com/article/uk-yemen-security/allies-of-yemen-houthis-seize-aden-airport-close-in-on-president-idUKKBN0ML0YM20150325

Alley, April Longley, “Yemen’s Multiple Crises,” *Journal of Democracy*, Vol. 21, No. 4, October 2010, pp. 72–86.

———, “Tracking the ‘Arab Spring’: Yemen Changes Everything . . . and Nothing,” *Journal of Democracy*, Vol. 24, No. 4, October 2013, pp. 74–85.

Ardemagni, Eleonora, “The UAE’s Security-Economic Nexus in Yemen,” Carnegie Endowment for International Peace, July 19, 2018. As of August 5, 2020: https://carnegieendowment.org/sada/76876

Basalmah, Badr, *Local Governance in Yemen: Challenges and Opportunities*, Berlin: Berghof Foundation, May 2018.

BBC, “President Hadi Leaves Yemen as Saudi-Led Raids Continue,” March 27, 2015.

———, “Yemen Crisis: Geneva Talks Fail to Produce Ceasefire,” June 19, 2015. As of August 3, 2020: https://www.bbc.com/news/world-middle-east-33205359

Biswell, Anthony, *Yemen Economic Bulletin: The War for Monetary Control Enters a Dangerous New Phase*, Sana’a, Yemen: Sana’a Center for Strategic Studies, January 21, 2020. As of September 20, 2020: https://sanaacenter.org/publications/analysis/8674

Bodine, Barbara K., “Yemen: Primer and Prescriptions,” *PRISM*, Vol. 1, No. 3, 2010, pp. 43–58.

Byman, Daniel, “Saudi Arabia and the United Arab Emirates Have a Disastrous Yemen Strategy,” Brookings Institution, July 17, 2018. As of September 25, 2020: https://www.brookings.edu/blog/order-from-chaos/2018/07/17/saudi-arabia-and-the-united-arab-emirates-have-a-disastrous-yemen-strategy/

Carapico, Sheila, and Jermera Rone, “Yemen: Human Rights in Yemen During and After the 1994 War,” *Human Rights Watch/Middle East*, Vol. 6, No. 1, 1994, pp. 1–32.

Carboni, Andrea, and Luca Nevola, "Inside Ibb: A Hotbed of Infighting in Houthi-Controlled Yemen," Armed Conflict Location and Event Data Project, October 3, 2019. As of July 21, 2020: https://acleddata.com/2019/10/03/inside-ibb-a-hotbed-of-infighting-in-houthi-controlled-yemen/

Craig, Iona, "Bombed into Famine: How Saudi Air Campaign Targets Yemen's Food Supplies," *The Guardian*, December 12, 2017. As of August 3, 2020: https://www.theguardian.com/world/2017/dec/12/bombed-into-famine-how-saudi-air-campaign-targets-yemens-food-supplies

Cumming-Bruce, Nick, "Yemen Agrees to Cease-Fire with Rebels as Peace Talks Begin," *New York Times*, December 15, 2015.

al-Dawsari, Nadwa, "Tribal Governance and Stability in Yemen," Carnegie Endowment for International Peace, April 24, 2012.

Day, Stephen W., "Why Yemen's Peace Talks Failed," *Washington Post*, July 7, 2015.

Donais, Timothy, "Empowerment or Imposition? Dilemmas of Local Ownership in Post-Conflict Peacebuilding Processes," *Peace and Change*, Vol. 34, No. 1, 2009, pp. 3–26.

Fahim, Kareem, and Saeed Al-Batati, "Yemen Peace Talks End with No End to Conflict," *New York Times*, December 20, 2015.

Feierstein, Gerald M., "Resolving the Conflict in Yemen: U.S. Interests, Risks, and Policy," testimony before the U.S. Senate Foreign Relations Committee on March 9, 2017, Washington, D.C.: Middle East Institute, 2017. As of December 7, 2020: https://mei.edu/publications/resolving-conflict-yemen-us-interests-risks-and-policy

———, "Yemen: The 60-Year War," in Paul Salem and Ross Harrison, eds., *Escaping the Conflict Trap: Toward Ending Civil Wars in the Middle East*, Washington, D.C.: Middle East Institute, 2019.

Gaston, Erica, *Process Lessons Learned in Yemen's National Dialogue*, Washington, D.C.: United States Institute of Peace, February 2014.

Gaston, Erica, and Nadwa al-Dawsari, *Dispute Resolution and Justice Provision in Yemen's Transition*, Washington, D.C.: United States Institute of Peace, April 2014.

Ghobari, Mohammed, "Houthi Rebels Sign Deal with Yemen Parties to Form New Government," Reuters, September 21, 2014.

Global Rights Compliance and World Peace Foundation, *Accountability for Mass Starvation: Starvation in Yemen*, Den Haag, Netherlands; Somerville, Mass., September 3, 2019. As of August 3, 2020:
https://reliefweb.int/sites/reliefweb.int/files/resources/Accountability for Starvation Crimes-Yemen.pdf

Gulf News, "Unity in Defeating Al Houthi Scourge," August 11, 2019. As of July 21, 2020:
https://gulfnews.com/opinion/editorials/unity-in-defeating-al-houthi-scourge-1.65758907

Al-Hadayani, Ali, "Sheikh Saleh Bin Fared: There Is an International and Regional Understanding for the Need to Form the Southern Transitional Council," Southern Transitional Council, 2018. As of July 20, 2020:
https://en.stcaden.com/news/7809

Hearst, David, "Yemen President Says UAE Acting Like Occupiers," *Middle East Eye*, May 12, 2017. As of July 21, 2020:
https://www.middleeasteye.net/news/exclusive-yemen-president-says-uae-acting-occupiers

Holden, Michael, "WFP Hopeful Yemen's 'Good' Houthis Will Prevail to Allow Food Aid Suspension to End," Reuters, June 21, 2019. As of August 3, 2020:
https://news.trust.org/item/20190621144339-o70g0

International Rescue Committee, *They Die of Bombs, We Die of Need: Impact of Collapsing Public Health Systems in Yemen*, New York, March 2018. As of August 3, 2020:
https://www.rescue.org/sites/default/files/document/2604/theydieofbombswedieofneedfinal.pdf

Jalal, Ibrahim, "Yemen's Stockholm Agreement One Year On: Imaginary Progress?" Middle East Institute, January 22, 2020a.

———, "From Stockholm to Riyadh: Breaking the Yemen Peace Process Deadlock," Middle East Institute, February 13, 2020b. As of August 3, 2020:
https://www.mei.edu/publications/stockholm-riyadh-breaking-yemen-peace-process-deadlock

Johnston, Trevor, Matthew Lane, Abigail Casey, Heather J. Williams, Ashley L. Rhoades, James Sladden, Nathan Vest, Jordan R. Reimer, and Ryan Haberman, *Could the Houthis Be the Next Hizballah? Iranian Proxy Development in Yemen and the Future of the Houthi Movement*, Santa Monica, Calif.: RAND Corporation, RR-2551-OSD, 2020. As of December 3, 2020:
https://www.rand.org/pubs/research_reports/RR2551.html

Jones, Sam, and Matthias Sulz, "Press Release: Over 100,000 Reported Killed in Yemen War," Armed Conflict Location and Event Data Project, October 31, 2019. As of August 3, 2020:
https://acleddata.com/2019/10/31/press-release-over-100000-reported-killed-in-yemen-war/

Kambeck, Jens, "Land Disputes in Yemen," in Helen Lackner, ed., *Why Yemen Matters: A Society in Transition*, London: Saqi Books, 2014.

Knights, Michael, and Alex Almeida, "The Saudi-UAE War Effort in Yemen (Part 1): Operation Golden Arrow in Aden," Washington Institute, August 10, 2015. As of July 21, 2020: https://www.washingtoninstitute.org/policy-analysis/view/the-saudi-uae-war-effort-in-yemen-part-1-operation-golden-arrow-in-aden

Lackner, Helen, "Yemen: Why the Riyadh Agreement Is Collapsing," European Council on Foreign Relations, February 3, 2020. As of July 21, 2020: https://www.ecfr.eu/article/commentary_yemen_why_the_riyadh_agreement_is_collapsing

Lackner, Helen, and Raiman Al-Hamdani, "War and Pieces: Political Divides in Southern Yemen," European Council on Foreign Relations, January 22, 2020. As of July 21, 2020: https://www.ecfr.eu/publications/summary/war_and_pieces_political_divides_in_southern_yemen

Lowcock, Mark, "Briefing to the Security Council on the Humanitarian Situation in Yemen," United Nations, Office for the Coordination of Humanitarian Affairs, February 18, 2020. As of August 3, 2020: https://reliefweb.int/report/yemen/under-secretary-general-humanitarian-affairs-and-emergency-relief-coordinator-mark-26

al-Madhaji, Maged, *How Yemen's Post-2011 Transitional Phase Ended in War*, Sana'a, Yemen: Sana'a Center for Strategic Studies, May 19, 2016. As of August 3, 2020: https://sanaacenter.org/publications/main-publications/39

Mazzetti, Mark, and David D. Kirkpatrick, "Saudi Arabia Leads Air Assault in Yemen," *New York Times*, March 25, 2015. As of July 21, 2020: https://www.nytimes.com/2015/03/26/world/middleeast/al-anad-air-base-houthis-yemen.html

Michael, Maggie, "UN Probes Corruption in Its Own Agencies in Yemen Aid Effort," Associated Press, August 5, 2019. As of August 3, 2020: https://apnews.com/dcf8914d99af49ef902c56c84823e30c

Middle East Eye, "Yemen's Rial Plummets as Government and Houthis Battle over Banknotes," January 9, 2020. As of August 3, 2020: https://www.middleeasteye.net/news/houthis-maintain-price-yemeni-currency-their-areas

Middle East Policy Council, "Yemen's Anti-Houthi Alliance Cracking from Within," August 20, 2019. As of July 21, 2020: https://mepc.org/commentary/yemens-anti-houthi-alliance-cracking-within

Miles, Tom, "Southern Yemenis Warn Exclusion from U.N. Peace Talks Could Trigger New Conflict," Reuters, March 1, 2019.

Nagi, Ahmed, “Mahra, Yemen: A Shadow Conflict Worth Watching,” Carnegie Middle East Center, 2020. As of August 5, 2020: https://carnegie-mec.org/2020/02/20/mahra-yemen-shadow-conflict-worth-watching-pub-80986

National Democratic Institute, *Yemen: Tribal Conflict Management Program Research Report*, Washington, D.C., 2007.

Paffenholz, Thania, and Nick Ross, “Inclusive Peace Processes—an Introduction,” presented at *Development Dialogue 2015*, Hubli, India, February 6–8, 2015.

———, “Inclusive Political Settlements: New Insights from Yemen’s National Dialogue,” *PRISM*, Vol. 6, No. 1, March 2016.

Parodi, Carlos A., Elizabeth Rexford, and Elizabeth Van Wie Davis, “The Silent Demise of Democracy: The Role of the Clinton Administration in the 1994 Yemeni Civil War,” *Arab Studies Quarterly*, Vol. 16, No. 4, 1994.

Perkins, Brian, “Saudi Arabia and the UAE in al-Mahra: Securing Interests, Disrupting Local Order, and Shaping a Southern Military,” *Terrorism Monitor* (Jamestown Foundation), March 1, 2019. As of August 5, 2020: https://jamestown.org/program/saudi-arabia-and-the-uae-in-al-mahra-securing-interests-disrupting-local-order-and-shaping-a-southern-military/

Potter, Christina, “Largest Cholera Outbreak on Record Continues,” Outbreak Observatory, January 16, 2020. As of September 25, 2020: https://www.outbreakobservatory.org/outbreakthursday-1/1/16/2020/large-cholera-outbreak-on-record-continues-in-yemen

Raghavan, Sudarsan, “In Ancient Yemeni City, Violence Turns Inward,” *Washington Post*, December 6, 2018. As of July 21, 2020: https://www.washingtonpost.com/news/world/wp/2018/12/06/feature/the-merchants-of-despair/

Raleigh, Clionadh, Andrew Linke, Håvard Hegre, and Joakim Karlsen, “Introducing ACLED—Armed Conflict Location and Event Data,” *Journal of Peace Research*, Vol. 47, No. 5, 2010, pp. 1–10.

Ramani, Samuel, “Iran’s Post-Conflict Vision in Yemen,” Carnegie Endowment for International Peace, December 11, 2019. As of August 5, 2020: https://carnegieendowment.org/sada/80557

Reinl, James, “Yemen Won’t See Peace Without Addressing Southern Demands: Separatist Leader,” *Middle East Eye*, December 15, 2018.

Reuters, "U.N.-Sponsored Peace Talks for Yemen," June 7, 2018. As of August 3, 2020: https://www.reuters.com/article/us-un-yemen-factbox/u-n-sponsored-peace-talks-for-yemen-idUSKCN1J31M9

———, "Yemeni Separatists Arrest Dozens of Government Loyalists in Aden," August 31, 2019. As of July 21, 2020: https://www.reuters.com/article/us-yemen-security-arrest/yemeni-separatists-arrest-dozens-of-government-loyalists-in-aden-idUSKCN1VL0AW

Robinson, Eric, P. Kathleen Frier, Kim Cragin, Melissa A. Bradley, Daniel Egel, Bryce Loidolt, and Paul S. Steinberg, *What Factors Cause Individuals to Reject Violent Extremism in Yemen?* Santa Monica, Calif.: RAND Corporation, RR-1727-OSD, 2017. As of December 8, 2020: https://www.rand.org/pubs/research_reports/RR1727.html

Salisbury, Peter, *Yemen: National Chaos, Local Order*, London: Chatham House, December 2017. As of August 3, 2020: https://www.chathamhouse.org/publication/yemen-national-chaos-local-order

———, *Yemen's Southern Powder Keg*, London: Chatham House, March 2018a.

———, "What Does the Stockholm Agreement Mean for Yemen?" *Washington Post*, December 21, 2018b. As of August 3, 2020: https://www.washingtonpost.com/news/monkey-cage/wp/2018/12/21/what-does-the-stockholm-agreement-mean-for-yemen/

Salmoni, Barak A., Bryce Loidolt, and Madeleine Wells, *Regime and Periphery in Northern Yemen: The Huthi Phenomenon*, Santa Monica, Calif.: RAND Corporation, MG-962-DIA, 2010. As of December 8, 2020: https://www.rand.org/pubs/monographs/MG962.html

Sana'a Center for Strategic Studies, "Yemen Economic Bulletin: How Currency Arbitrage Has Reduced the Funds Available to Address the Humanitarian Crisis," September 6, 2017. As of August 3, 2020: https://sanaacenter.org/publications/analysis/4740

———, "Yemen's War Profiteers Are Potential Spoilers of the Peace Process," December 11, 2018. As of August 3, 2020: https://sanaacenter.org/publications/the-yemen-review/6732

———, *War's Elusive End—the Yemen Annual Review 2019*, Sana'a, Yemen, 2020. As of July 20, 2020: https://sanaacenter.org/publications/the-yemen-review/8923

Save the Children, "Yemen: Hunger and Disease Could Kill at Least 50,000 Children This Year, More If Aid Blockade Continues," press release, November 15, 2017. As of December 8, 2020: https://www.savethechildren.org/us/about-us/media-and-news/2017-press-releases/yemen--hunger-and-disease-could-kill-at-least-50-000-children-th

———, "Yemen: 85,000 Children May Have Died from Starvation Since Start of War," November 20, 2018. As of December 8, 2020: https://www.savethechildren.org/us/about-us/media-and-news/2018-press-releases/yemen-85000-children-may-have-died-from-starvation

Schmitz, Charles, *Yemen's National Dialogue*, Washington, D.C.: Middle East Institute, February 2014.

Thiel, Tobias, "Yemen's Imposed Federal Boundaries," Middle East Research and Information Project, July 20, 2015. As of December 8, 2020: https://merip.org/2015/07/yemens-imposed-federal-boundaries

United Nations, "UN Officials Welcome Cessation of Hostilities," *UN News*, April 11, 2016a. As of July 21, 2020: https://news.un.org/en/story/2016/04/526392-yemen-un-officials-welcome-cessation-hostilities

———, "Ban Condemns Reported Coalition Airstrike on Rural Hospital That Leaves 11 Dead," *UN News*, August 16, 2016b. As of July 21, 2020: https://news.un.org/en/story/2016/08/536712-yemen-ban-condemns-reported-coalition-airstrike-rural-hospital-leaves-11-dead

———, "Yemen: UN Envoy Urges 72-Hour Extension of Ceasefire," *UN News*, October 22, 2016c. As of August 3, 2020: https://news.un.org/en/story/2016/10/543502-yemen-un-envoy-urges-72-hour-extension-ceasefire

———, "10 Million Yemenis 'One Step Away from Famine,' UN Food Relief Agency Calls for 'Unhindered Access' to Frontline Regions," *UN News*, March 26, 2019. As of August 3, 2020: https://news.un.org/en/story/2019/03/1035501

United Nations Department of Global Communications, "Regular Press Briefing by the Information Service: Syria, Yemen, World Migration Trends," November 15, 2019. As of August 3, 2020: https://reliefweb.int/report/yemen/regular-press-briefing-information-service-syria-yemen-world-migration-trends-15

United Nations Financial Tracking Service, "Yemen 2019," webpage, undated. As of August 3, 2020:
https://fts.unocha.org/appeals/675/summary

United Nations Human Rights Council, *Annual Report of the United Nations High Commissioner for Human Rights and Reports of the Office of the High Commissioner and the Secretary-General*, Geneva, August 9, 2019.

United Nations Office for the Coordination of Humanitarian Affairs, "Yemen—Nutrition Smart Survey," data set, 2019. As of August 3, 2020:
https://data.humdata.org/dataset/yemen-nutrition-smart-survey

V TLR, "Yemen: Questions About an Aid System," Fondation Médecins Sans Frontières, Centre de Réflexion sur l'Action et les Savoirs Humanitaires, June 20, 2019.

World Health Organization, "Cholera Situation in Yemen, December 2019," December 31, 2019. As of August 3, 2020:
https://reliefweb.int/report/yemen/cholera-situation-yemen-december-2019

World Bank, *The Republic of Yemen: Unlocking the Potential for Economic Growth*, Washington, D.C., October 2015. As of October 28, 2020:
https://openknowledge.worldbank.org/bitstream/handle/10986/23660/Yemen00Republi00for0economic0growth.pdf

Yemen Central Statistical Organization, "Yemen—CSO 2017 Population Projections by Governorate & District, Sex & Age Disaggregated," data set, Data.world, last updated 2019. As of January 4, 2020:
https://data.world/ocha-yemen/8ded1878-b737-4922-adf4-05216bd46674